INDIA'S G20 LEGACY

SHAPING A NEW WORLD ORDER

TAKING G20 TO NEW HEIGHTS

"Together we will make the G20 inclusive, ambiguous, action-oriented and decisive. Over the past year, together we have realized that vision.

Together we have taken G20 to new heights.

Amidst a world fraught with distrust and challenges, it is mutual trust that binds us, connects us to each other.

In this one year, we have believed in "One Earth, One Family, One Future." And, we have shown unity and cooperation beyond controversies.

I can never forget that moment when all of us in Delhi unanimously welcomed the African Union to the G20.

The message of inclusivity that G20 has given to the whole world is unprecedented. It is a matter of pride for India that Africa has got a voice during its Presidency.

In this one year, the whole world has also heard the echo of the Global South in G20. In the Voice of Global South Summit last week, about 130 countries have wholeheartedly appreciated the decisions taken at the New Delhi G20 Summit.

The G20 has emphasized the adoption of a human-centric approach while supporting innovation and digital technology. The G20 has renewed faith in multilateralism.

Together we have given direction to multilateral development banks and global governance reforms.

And along with these, during the Presidency of India, G20 has got the recognition of People's 20. Crores of ordinary citizens of India joined G20, and celebrated it as a festival.

Today, India is prepared to walk together shoulder to shoulder, to meet the expectations of the world and of humanity.

The 21st century world will have to give top priority to the concerns of the Global South moving forward."

(Excerpts from Prime Minister Narendra Modi's speech at the Virtual G20 summit on November 22, 2023)

INDIA'S G20 LEGACY

SHAPING A NEW WORLD ORDER

Editor

Manish Chand

PENTAGON PRESS LLP

First published in 2024 by

PENTAGON PRESS LLP
206, Peacock Lane, Shahpur Jat
New Delhi-110049, India
Contact: 011-64706243

Typeset in Adobe Garamond, 11.5 Point
Printed by Aegean Offset Printers, Greater Noida, U.P.

ISBN 978-81-968722-4-3

www.pentagonpress.in

To My Late Father Shri Umesh Chand,
who always believed in me,
and the rise of India

CONTENTS

FOREWORD: Harsh Vardhan Shringla   xi

INTRODUCTION: Manish Chand   xv

SECTION 1: DECODING THE LEGACY

1. Reviving Global South and Restoring Multilateralism   3
   Dr S. Jaishankar

2. Prioritising Africa and Global South at G20   6
   Dr. G.N.M. Pandor

3. India's G20 Presidency and Rise of the Global South   10
   Amitabh Kant

4. Inclusive Solutions for an Inclusive World   22
   Harsh Vardhan Shringla

5. India's Moment: Forging a Value-based Future   30
   Sujan R. Chinoy

6. G20 India: A Diplomatic and Organisational Feat   35
   Muktesh Pardeshi

7. Shared Priorities: From Indian G20 Presidency to Italian G7
   Presidency   43
   His Excellency Vincenzo de Luca

8. Shared Legacy: Ending Poverty and Reforming
   Global Governance   47
   His Excellency Kenneth Felix Haczynski da Nobrega

9. Vasudhaiva Kutumbakam: A Framework for Global Cooperation   53
Arvind Gupta

10. Raising the Bar for Women-led Development in G20   58
Lakshmi Puri

11. Global Geopolitics: India's Role as a Consensus Builder   66
D.B. Venkatesh Varma

SECTION 2: GLOBAL SOUTH AND AFRICA

12. Africa G20 Moment   75
Anil Sooklal

13. Africa, India, South Africa and the Global South in G20   81
Elizabeth Sidiropoulos

14. Delhi's G20 Legacy: Empowering and Elevating Africa   85
Rajiv Bhatia

15. Rise of the Global South: A Catalyst for a New World Order   94
Manish Chand

16. Global South: Shaping Global Governance   101
Anil Wadhwa

17. African Union's Effective Participation in the G20   109
Pradeep S. Mehta

18. The African Continent: A Voice, an Opportunity, and a Greater Role   117
Pamla Gopaul, Kennedy Mbeva and Reuben Makomere

19. Africa Factor in India's G20 Presidency   125
Gurjit Singh

SECTION 3: BROADENING THE AGENDA

20. India's Legacy: Promoting Environmentally Responsible and Sustainable Development   133
Vibha Dhawan

21. Harnessing Trade and Investment for Inclusive Prosperity   138
    Mohan Kumar

22. India-US Partnership and India's G20 Success   144
    Mukesh Aghi

23. Global Partnership for Sustainable Development:
    The New Delhi Summit and Beyond   150
    Nagesh Kumar

24. India's G20 Imprint: Deepening Civil Society Connect   158
    Vijay Nambiar

25. Inclusive Development and G20: Progress and Prospects   172
    Nitya Mohan Khemka

26. A Multipolar World: Forging G20 Unity to Accelerate UN
    Reforms and SDGs   180
    Anna-Katharina Hornidge and Alma Wisskirchen

27. Integrating Cultural Outreach in G20   185
    Abhay K.

    About the Contributors   196

    Acknowledgements   205

    Index   207

FOREWORD

HARSH VARDHAN SHRINGLA

India's year-long G20 presidency, which concluded on November 30, 2023 has left an indelible imprint and a lasting legacy. For years to come, India's G20 will influence how the world addresses global challenges. The presidency was historic and transformational. It successfully bridged geopolitical divides to forge global unity, pivoted on the mantra of 'One World, One Earth, and One Future.' The G20 New Delhi Leaders' Declaration, achieved after hundreds of days and hours of intense negotiations, was historic and underscored the triumph of diplomacy and consensus over polarisation and politicking.

India's G20 presidency, guided by Prime Minister Narendra Modi's 'inclusive, ambitious, decisive, and action-oriented' vision, was an exceptional demonstration of India's best practices, values, and traditions. Guided by the ancient wisdom of *Vasudhaiva Kutumbakam*, India's year at the helm of the G20 saw the world's most powerful multilateral grouping undergo a significant transformation, most significantly in terms of the space given to the Global South.

Driven by Prime Minister Modi's vision of taking G20 events across India, the G20 was transformed from an annual event into a mass movement, shifting the G20's GDP-focused view of the world into a human-centric one.

While millions of words have been written, we need a holistic understanding and appreciation of India's G20 legacy and how it will influence the evolution of multilateralism and help shape a more inclusive world. This book, '*India's G20 Legacy: Shaping a New World Order*' edited by journalist, author and publisher Manish Chand, is therefore timely and a valuable guide to decoding India's G20 presidency which has generated unprecedented international attention. Manish Chand has been ardently tracking India's tryst with the G20 presidency much before it all started and this deep involvement and understanding shows in how this book has been curated and edited. This insightful book delves beyond the headlines, offering diverse perspectives, fresh insights, and critical evaluations of India's transformative presidency. From the unexpected outcomes of policy shifts to the hidden gems of cultural diplomacy, Manish Chand's curated collection unveils the nuanced story of India's leadership and its lasting influence on the evolution of multilateralism.

The book's most significant strength lies in presenting a diversity of viewpoints and perspectives on India's G20 presidency by those who were directly involved with shaping it as well as veteran diplomats, practitioners, academics and authors from India and the rest of the world. With the baton passing on to Brazil in 2024-2025 and South Africa in 2025-2026, the book illuminates the outcomes India's G20 presidency has for successive presidencies of the Global South and the future evolution of this crucial global grouping.

In a world fractured by conflict and shrouded in the fog of isolationist ideologies, 'India's G20 Legacy' shines as a beacon of hope. Through the vivid lens of India's G20 presidency, the book eloquently underscores the vital role of bridge-building and consensus-building in navigating the tumultuous waters of our times. Its message resonates particularly with Brazil, as it embarks on its own G20 leadership journey. India's story offers a roadmap for how to elevate the G20 beyond mere economic discussions and connect it to the aspirations of the people, paving the way for a more inclusive and equitable future for all.

For me, and many would agree with it, the most important legacy of India's G20 presidency was its overarching focus on inclusivity, both domestically and internationally. Inclusivity was the prime focus in India's G20, not just in terms of priorities, but also through organization. Prime Minister Modi recognized the power of using India's G20 platform to celebrate the nation's diversity, and illustrate how this very diversity could become a unifying factor on the global stage.

As I have written in my chapter on this theme in the book, India's G20

Presidency exemplified how a developing nation at the forefront of the G20 not only elevates the voices of the Global South but also empowers emerging economies to take a leading role in confronting pressing global issues. From making the G20 more inclusive by welcoming the African Union as a permanent member to tackling the climate crisis, addressing the post-COVID deceleration of Sustainable Development Goals and navigating the complexities of the Ukraine conflict, India's chairmanship showcased the power of shared purpose. It demonstrated that India, as the G20 Chair, not only championed policies aligned with its interests but also fostered increased multilateral cooperation.

India's G20 leadership wasn't just a moment, it was a movement. By firmly believing in inclusivity and demonstrating leadership by example, India ignited a spark of hope in a world yearning for a more equitable future. As we face the cascading challenges of our time, the spirit of '*Vasudhaiva Kutumbakam*' demands to be heard louder than ever. Thus, this book, rich with the transformational aspects of India's legacy, isn't just a testament to the past; it's a clarion call to action.

Harsh Vardhan Shringla
Harsh Vardhan Shringla served as the Chief Coordinator of India's
G20 Presidency and the Foreign Secretary of India

INTRODUCTION
Unpacking India's G20 Legacy

MANISH CHAND

'Legacy' means a bequest or a gift that is passed on. Beyond the literal meaning, 'legacy' symbolises leaving behind pathways for future generations and providing guidance and inspiration for them. Whichever way one looks at it, India's year-long G20 presidency was pathbreaking and transformative in myriad ways, leaving a lasting legacy by paving the way for shaping an inclusive and human-centric world order.

India's G20 presidency has been widely praised in academic and strategic circles for reinvigorating multilateralism and bridging divides in a ceaselessly conflicted world. This book takes a critical look at different aspects of India's G20 presidency and the key outcomes of the New Delhi summit in September 2023, which has set the stage for a new world order reflective of new power shifts and aspirations of those who have been marginalised in the global system.

This book comprises original perspectives and behind-the-scenes narratives by key figures in India's G20 Secretariat, who proactively crafted the agenda and worked tirelessly to shape the outcomes that will continue to create ripples in the years to come. This volume also includes commentaries and disquisitions by eminent diplomats, scholars, and experts, who take the long view to define and frame India's G20 legacy.

This book is divided into three sections: (I) Decoding the Legacy; (II) Global South the Africa; and (III) Broadening the Agenda. The first section comprises essays and commentaries by key personalities involved in conceptualising and steering India's G20 presidency. The contributors include India's G20 Sherpa Amitabh Kant; India's then Chief G20 Coordinator Harsh Vardhan Shringla; and Muktesh Pardeshi, Special

Secretary in the MEA, who supervised organisational and logistical aspects relating to various G20 meetings. This volume also includes an insightful chapter by Italy's Ambassador to India Vincenzo de Luca, which draws connections between India's G20 presidency and Italy's G7 presidency. Brazil's Ambassador to India Kenneth Felix Haczynski da Nobrega has contributed an article that maps the continuity between key priorities of India's G20 presidency with the agenda of Brazil's G20 presidency.

The second section on 'Global South and Africa' includes commentaries on how the inclusion of the AU as the 21st permanent member of the G20 has made the grouping more representative and future-ready, unveiling an emerging narrative of South-South solidarity. Prominent scholars and experts from Africa and India have contributed their insights and analyses to this section.

The third section on 'Broadening the Agenda' includes different thematic strands of India's G20 agenda, encompassing trade, green development, culture, civil society, and reforming global governance architecture.

With the baton passing on to Brazil in 2023-2024 and South Africa in 2024-2025, this book encapsulates major thematic strands that frame the legacy of India's G20 presidency and the lessons it holds for successive presidencies of the Global South and the future evolution of this crucial global grouping.

Hope, Healing and Harmony

A year is too short to radically reconfigure the world order, but India's G20 presidency has raised the bar for what innovative diplomacy can do to shape a world order that is more sensitive to the aspirations of developing countries and the poorest of the poor – what Prime Minister Narendra Modi described as "leaving no one behind." To understand the nature and compass of India's legacy, one has to go back to the time when the G20 baton was formally passed to New Delhi on 1 December 2022. India assumed the G20 mantle in a badly fractured and divisive world, marked by four Ps – poly-crisis, paranoia, polarisation, and perplexity. The Ukraine conflict had intensified geopolitical divisions, and consensus was proving to be the elusive Holy Grail.

The geopolitical rivalry between the world's two powers, the USA and China, was escalating, and questions were being raised more vocally than ever about the capacity of global institutions to mitigate financial distress in large parts of the developing world that were suffering from the after-effects of supply chain disruptions and climate catastrophes. The spirit of multilateralism was almost dead; it was each country for itself. It was against this gloom-and-doom backdrop that India's G20 presidency, framed around the Vedic ethos of '*Vasudhaiva Kutumbakam*' (One Earth, One Family, One Future), emerged as a beacon of 'Healing, Hope and Harmony.' In his very first speech after formally assuming the G20 presidency, Prime Minister Narendra Modi underscored that "India's G20 agenda will be inclusive, ambitious, action-oriented, and decisive," and exhorted the world to "work together to shape a new paradigm of human-centric globalisation." Infusing hope in a stressed and conflicted world can, therefore, be considered the first strand of India's G20 legacy.

Inclusion: Global South and Africa

The formal inclusion of the African Union as the 21st permanent member of the G20 on Day 1 of the New Delhi summit will go down in history as India's enduring legacy and signature achievement. Inside the newly-created Bharat Mandapam, the majestic setting for the New Delhi summit, history was made as Prime Minister Narendra Modi invited AU Chairperson, Comorian President Azali Assoumani, to occupy a seat at the G20 high table. PM Modi hugging President Assoumani is one of the iconic images of the Delhi summit – it triggered applause across capitals in African countries and the developing world. With this historic step, the G20's trajectory has been irreversibly changed. Issues and interests of the Global South are now expected to find greater resonance in the future summits of the G20. In this respect, India's G20 presidency marks a turning point for the ascendance of the Global South in the multilateral agenda. Four successive G20 presidencies of emerging powers, including Indonesia, India, Brazil, and South Africa, are poised to be game-changers, shaping the future evolution of the world's most representative global grouping. India also ensured the highest African participation in the G20 to date, by including Mauritius, Egypt, Nigeria, AU Chair Comoros, and AUDA-NEPAD as invitees to the forum.

The primacy of the Global South in India's G20 presidency was crystallised in the two editions of the 'Voice of Global South Summit,' which India hosted in January 2023 and the final month of its G20 presidency in November the same year. Going by an enthusiastic response, the 'Voice of the South Summit' is likely to become a permanent feature in the future presidencies by the G20 countries.

With the geopolitical power dynamics shifting in favour of non-Western developing countries, the G20 summit in New Delhi underlined the West's willingness to provide a greater say for the Global South in shaping the international agenda.

Broadening the Agenda

The summit's key outcomes bear India's imprint. They included the adoption of the G20 Action Plan for accelerating SDGs, the acceptance of the Green Development Compact, the transformative use of technologies to advance financial inclusion, the strengthening of multilateral development banks (MDBs) to make them bigger and better, the adoption of LiFE (Lifestyle for the Environment) principles for sustainable development and the launch of a financial inclusion action plan, and productivity gains through Digital Public Infrastructure.

The New Delhi summit also marked a turning point in international efforts to curb global warming by raising the targets for climate finance. Developed countries have expressed their willingness for the first time to fulfill their commitment of 100 billion dollars for climate finance. The launch of the Global Biofuel Alliance will accelerate global efforts to meet net zero emission targets by facilitating trade in biofuels derived from various sources, including plant and animal wastes.

People's G20

Opinions may differ on this, but if one were to take the long view, mass participation in G20 meetings across India, which brought an elite forum closer to ordinary people, can be considered a signature achievement of the country's G20 presidency. The transformation of the G20 into a people's festival through large-scale civil society participation in the G20 meetings held across India has left an example for succeeding presidencies to deepen 'people connect' with G20. By the time India's G20 presidency term ended, over 220 meetings had been organised across 60 cities in all the 28 states and eight Union territories. During the 12 months of India's G20 presidency, over 100,000 participants from around 125 nationalities visited a new incredible India that effortlessly blended the culture and history of a civilizational state with the enterprise and innovation of a rising global power.

The Road Ahead

Above all, the G20 presidency sealed India's status as a rising global power and its capacity to build bridges between rival power centres, which were reflected in the consensus on the deeply contentious Ukraine issue. Top world leaders, including leaders of the G20 countries, have hailed the summit as a grand success, which restores global confidence in multilateralism and buttresses the G20's position as the world's most representative leaders' forum. In a triumph for Indian diplomacy and bridge-building skills, the 83-para-New Delhi Declaration succeeded in forging a consensus formulation on the Ukraine crisis by finding the middle ground between the G7 countries and Russia.

At the summit, Prime Minister Narendra Modi pitched strongly for the expansion of the UN Security Council and reforms of global institutions to reflect the world's 'new realities.' Brazilian President Luiz Inácio Lula da Silva, who took over the G20 presidency from PM Modi, backed global governance reforms saying the UNSC needed new developing countries as permanent and non-permanent members to gain political strength and greater representation for emerging countries at the World Bank and the IMF. The G20 summit in Delhi, with a strong focus on the Global South, has generated additional momentum for the reform of global governance institutions, thereby charting the way for a new world order.

Looking ahead, India/Bharat's G20 presidency will be remembered for making the G20 a catalytic agent for people's empowerment and the creation of a human-centric and balanced world order. Being human-centric means going beyond ideological binaries and the North-South divide to engineer tangible improvement in people's lives and to fashion a more caring, compassionate and inclusive world order. At this point, some caveats are in order: This book is not an uncritical panegyric to India's G20 presidency, but includes analytical expositions of the power of multilateralism in a fractured and divisive world. It vividly underscores the compelling need for the world to act in the spirit of 'One Earth, One Family and One Future.'

We hope that this volume will ignite debate and ideation on the future of the G20 and the prospects of a more inclusive G20, which is in tune with vital interests and priorities of the Global South, a process that acquired an unstoppable momentum during India's G20 presidency, and is expected to be carried forward by both developed and developing countries of the G20 grouping. The role of leaders in driving global diplomacy cannot be overstated. In this regard, Prime Minister Modi and his team invested unprecedented capital – political, financial and diplomatic – to make this once-in-20-year presidency a huge success, thereby sealing India's stature as a major global power and a bridge-builder in a conflicted world. The only way to address global challenges effectively is to focus on what unites us, not what divides us, said PM Modi in his message to the G20 foreign ministers in New Delhi. The ancient Sanskrit saying '*Sarvajan Hitaya, Sarvajan Sukhaya*' (For the welfare of all, for the happiness of all) crystallises the essence of India's G20 presidency and shows the way forward.

SECTION 1

DECODING THE LEGACY

Reviving Global South and Restoring Multilateralism

Dr S. Jaishankar

India took over its G20 presidency in the backdrop of a deep divide in the international polity, the devastation caused by the Covid pandemic, increasing stresses on global food, fertilizer and energy security, and an intractable debt crisis. This context made us conscious of the great responsibility of assuming the G20 presidency.

In fulfilling that task, India's anchor was the Global South. Its voices inspired our priorities, fuelled our efforts and galvanized a path-breaking consensus in a very diverse grouping. At the first summit, we heard your concerns about the rising impact of climate change, tightening global markets, and an increasingly conditional and narrowing global resource mechanisms. Since then, conflicts around the world have only further exacerbated humanitarian challenges. Climate change continues to have a disproportionate impact on Least Developed Countries and Small Island Developing States. Prospects for a global economic recovery remain challenging.

Global Development Agenda

The New Delhi G20 Summit refocused that body and the world looks at the global development agenda, linking it to every major agenda before us today, be it climate change, energy transitions, or technological transformations. Even the contours of the climate debate were redefined by anchoring it in a holistic narrative, looking also at the demand side of polluting our environment. We democratized the narrative by bringing focus on individual actions through the LiFE initiative i.e. Lifestyle for Environment initiative.

We imbued the Energy Transitions discussions by emphasizing that it must be a globally just one. We highlighted that the localization of SDGs needs to be accompanied with the internationalization of its resourcing. We created templates for progress in SDGs by harnessing digital tools and infrastructure. And finally, we have brought back G20's focus to its original mandate which is Sustainable Development. This is demonstrated amongst others by the consensus on the G20 Green Development Pact (GDP). It is about achieving major global agendas in an interconnected manner.

Reforming Multilateralism

The New Delhi Summit also highlighted the need for restoring trust in multilateralism. There is a strong expectation in the Global South, which must be further built upon. By securing permanent membership for the African Union in the G20, we have shown that global groupings are amenable to change. The same spirit must now pervade the reform of the United Nations. Prime Minister Modi firmly believes that the success of our G20 presidency is the success of the Global South.

The endeavours undertaken during India's G20 presidency, under our theme of 'One Earth, One Family, One Future', will continue to be heard as we work to realize our vision for a world, where truly no one is left behind anywhere in the world. Recognising our shared past, the Global South will continue to make efforts for One Earth and to strengthen the voices of the developing countries.

Together, for Everyone's Growth

As One Family, the Global South will continue to act with everyone's interests in mind and drive transformations while building synergies. Creating our One Future will need making international institutions future-ready and increasing their effectiveness, and enhancing the representative character of their decisions. The theme of the "Voice of Global South Summit," which is "Together for Everyone's Growth, Together for Everyone's Trust" is a mantra for our future actions in this direction.

(This article is based on opening Remarks by India's External Affairs Minister Dr. S. Jaishankar at the Foreign Ministers' Session-II of the 2nd Voice of Global South Summit, hosted by India, on November 17, 2023)

2

Prioritising Africa and Global South at G20

DR. G.N.M. PANDOR

The G20 has become one of the pre-eminent global agenda-setting bodies in international relations outside of formal UN structures. Not only does the G20 serve as the premier economic forum for international cooperation but it also is an important vehicle to advance Africa's development priorities. The themes India has chosen for its G20 Presidency this year place the Global South at the centre of development planning. Accelerating progress on the UN Sustainable Development Goals is a key priority of India's presidency, and reflects South Africa's policy goals which are in harmony with this year's G20 Action Plan.

India's proposals of a Green Development Pact for a sustainable future and its proposed reforms of multilateral institutions for the 21st century reflect our own foreign policy priorities.

Digital Power

India is committed to bridging the digital divide through technology transfer and digital transformation. South Africa believes that If digital architecture is made widely accessible, it can bring about socioeconomic transformation, and the use of digital technologies can become a force multiplier in the fight against poverty.

Harnessing data for development is critical for providing greater access to the internet and improving digital skills. As India's G20 Sherpa Amitabh Kant has said, "There are 400 million people who do not have a digital identity, 200 million people do not have a bank account, and 133 countries do not even have fast payments. This is a massive opportunity to use technology to transform the world."

Green Finance

Fast-tracking the delivery of climate finance is a high priority for India's G20 presidency. It is the perspective of both India and South Africa that developing countries require substantive climate finance to meet their ambitious goals, and developed countries need to lead the mobilisation of resources.

The G20 summit in Bali last year agreed to expedite the delivery of climate finance to developing countries and work on an ambitious New Collective Quantified Goal of climate finance from US$100 billion per year to support developing countries. The Bali Declaration urged developed countries to at least double their collective provision of climate finance for adaptation to developing countries, from 2019 levels, by 2025, in the context of achieving a balance between mitigation and adaptation. There needs to be concrete action from developed countries in terms of climate finance and strengthening the capacity of developing countries to combat climate change. We must also work with G20 countries to scale up the deployment of zero and low-emission power generation, including renewable energy.

Under the Indian Presidency, there is also a focus on enhancing food security, and the need to mobilise the international community to maintain the supply of both fertilisers and grains. Given the non-renewal of the grain deal, whereby Russia was asked to extend the agreement that enabled Ukraine to export grain from its Black Sea ports, this issue is all the more urgent.

India has emphasised the fact that developed countries need to honour their financial commitments to developing countries most in need. Through its laudable support for the Debt Service Suspension Initiative, the G20 attempted to provide relief to developing countries, but the results were below expectations. Not only have developed countries not met their commitments to the developing world, they are trying consistently to shift responsibility to the Global South. We hope that this year's G20 will bring about more tangible commitments in this regard.

We commend India for its numerous active ministerial meetings that have interrogated all of these issues, and for the consistent contact among the G20 Sherpas.

It's Time for Africa

South Africa also welcomes the Indian Presidency's call for the G20 to accept the African Union as a permanent member of the G20. We believe there is a need for Africa to be fully involved in the decision-making processes on global political, economic, financial, security, environmental and health governance. India, as an emerging global power, is well placed to ensure that the core interests of the developing world, including Africa, are a priority during its presidency. Africa will look to India to ensure that its socio-economic regeneration, as articulated in Agenda 2063, receives the attention it deserves within the G20 this year.

The G20 remains the best forum to pursue the reform of financial and economic multilateral institutions. Making global financial governance institutions more democratic and representative given the ongoing shifts in the world order is a major priority for this year's G20. The World Bank and IMF need to be more representative to be relevant, and developing countries need greater decision-making power.

Multilateral institutions and international financing institutions, including development banks, need to reform urgently given the rise of emerging economies. A country like Ethiopia – home to more than 100 million people – controls only 0.09% of the votes in the IMF, while the US has a vote share of 16%. This needs to change.

In recent times, the agenda of the G20 has expanded beyond economic and financial issues, and now encompasses issues of peace and security. The G20 is not a substitute for the UN system and should remain an economic development forum and refrain from centering peace and security issues in the forum.

Bridging Divides

The war in Ukraine must not be allowed to divert from the core objectives of the G20. The Global South is concerned at the possibility of the G20 agenda being derailed by the ongoing tensions between Russia and the West. This was the primary challenge that Indonesia faced throughout its presidency and at the Summit itself. There is a need to bridge divides between countries which are polarised over the Ukraine war, so that the G20 can focus on the challenges for which it was created – accelerating Sustainable Development Goals (SDGs), reviving economic growth, and generating the much-needed climate finance.

The model of rotation in the presidency of the G20 allows countries of the South to exercise leadership, and India's Presidency this year, the Brazilian Presidency in 2024, and South Africa's Presidency in 2025 will prioritise the global South's development priorities. The Johannesburg II Declaration adopted at the recent XV BRICS Summit underscored the importance of the G20 in continuing to play the role of the premier multilateral forum in international economic and financial cooperation to jointly seek solutions to global challenges.

3

India's G20 Presidency and Rise of the Global South

AMITABH KANT

An enduring memory from India's G20 presidency that will forever linger in my memory is the powerful image of the Prime Minister embracing the President of Comoros and Chair of the African Union (AU), welcoming the AU as a permanent member of the G20. This single gesture transformed the G20 into a more representative and inclusive body, incorporating over 1 billion people from Africa. Achieving this milestone required a year of dedicated efforts by India, overcoming challenges and standing firm on the inclusion of the AU, despite competing interests from other regions. While several nations vouched for ASEAN, and others championed alternative regional entities as full G20 members, India steadfastly advocated for the inclusion of the AU.

Victory for Global South

Prior to this moment, Prime Minister Modi convened the first-of-its-kind Voice of the Global South Summit, in which 125 leaders from the loose geographical grouping had come together to discuss their shared interests. Aligning with their shared priorities, he penned letters to fellow leaders, underscoring the imperative for the AU to secure a permanent seat at India's G20 table.

With the permanent inclusion of the AU, announced on 9 September 2023 during the New Delhi G20 Summit, India transformed the G20 into a substantially more inclusive institution, now encapsulating nearly 90 per cent of the global population. This expansion extends to covering approximately three-fourths of global trade, establishing the G20 as a body representing close to 80 per cent of the world's population. India's advocacy has undeniably elevated inclusive representation in the G20 for ever.

The New Delhi Leaders' Declaration stands as a significant document in the history of multilateralism, representing the resolute voice and aspirations of the Global South. This hard-won victory reflects years of persistent efforts, where every word and paragraph symbolizes the challenges overcome.

At the outset of India's G20 presidency, we faced a world grappling with significant challenges. In the post-COVID era, nearly 200 million people fell below the poverty line, and almost 100 million lost their jobs. A global recession loomed, with Germany already in its throes, and 75 countries facing a burgeoning debt crisis. Amidst these issues, we navigated the complexities of climate action, climate finance, and the enduring conflict in Europe spanning over a year.

Yet, in the face of these crises, we embraced them as opportunities, echoing the Prime Minister's vision of a presidency marked by inclusivity, decisiveness, ambition, and action orientation.

Examining the New Delhi Leaders' Declaration reveals a comprehensive document comprising 83 paragraphs, 87 outcomes, approximately 112 attached documents, and a total of about 205 outcomes and documents. Remarkably, every aspect has been crafted without reservations, dissents, footnotes, or objections from any country, underscoring the achievement of unanimous consensus.

India's G20 legacy is a testament to our ability to thrust multilateralism back into the spotlight, revitalizing it from a receding position. Within this renewed focus, we elevated the development agenda of the Global South, emphasizing climate action, climate finance, and reforming multilateral institutions, including development banks and financial architecture. Additionally, our G20 presidency underscored the significance of technological transformation and digital public infrastructure while giving prominence to women-led development, a crucial element for global progress.

In demonstrating the potential of an emerging market such as India to bring not only the G7, but also other emerging markets like Russia and China to centre stage, we showcased our capacity to drive consensus in an increasingly divided world. India played a pivotal role in uniting diverse stakeholders, fostering collaboration, and advancing the cause of a multilateralism that is effective, up-to-date, and inclusive.

Key Priorities

When looking at our primary objectives, it is crucial to recognize that the G20, fundamentally an economic entity, distinguishes itself from geopolitical bodies like the United Nations and the UN Security Council. The G20 originated from the Finance Ministers and Central Bank Governors Forum, evolving in 2008 under President Bush's foresight. Recognizing the imperative to spur global growth, he facilitated the G20's transition from a finance-centric platform to a leader-driven forum. Since that pivotal moment, the G20's trajectory has been steered by leaders. Despite this evolution, the G20's core significance remains rooted in addressing growth and development issues on a global scale.

However, the Russia-Ukraine war proved to be a sticking point for many countries, given its far-reaching implications on essential commodities like food, fuel, and fertilizers. In 2023, during the G20 discussions in Indonesia, the spotlight shifted decisively towards geopolitics, resulting in a split para in the final declaration. India's mandate was difficult, but decisive: We needed to bring the focus back on development, and spotlight the concerns of the most vulnerable populations.

Robust, Sustainable, and Inclusive Growth

When reflecting on India's G20 priorities, our primary focus has been on fostering robust, sustainable, and inclusive growth. We firmly believe that sustained global growth is paramount; without it, the impetus for investments, trade, and overall prosperity falters. A substantial part of our discourse focused on the crucial facet of growth, with particular emphasis on liberalizing trade. Acknowledging historical patterns post-pandemics, marked by five to six years of protectionism, we underscored the importance of countering such tendencies to ensure accelerated and unhindered global growth.

The transformative power of trade in uplifting populations from poverty is evident, and India's own experience attests to this truth. However, the current global trend towards protectionism poses a significant challenge to trade dynamics worldwide. Such protectionist tendencies threaten to impede trade flows and hinder the upward trajectory of emerging markets, making the task of propelling growth much more difficult. Consequently, we knew that our discussions within the G20 must place a spotlight on fostering growth, recognizing it as the linchpin for overcoming these challenges.

Through a strategic approach, we directed our attention to the Global South, particularly noteworthy given that 80 per cent of this year's growth emerged from this region. Looking forward, the projections from the IMF and World Bank underscore the pivotal role of emerging markets, expected to contribute 70 per cent of global growth in the next two decades. This imperative necessitates a recalibration of multilateral financial institutions and development banks to align with and expedite this emerging-market-led growth.

Reforming Multilateralism

Further, it is crucial to acknowledge that the current institutional framework traces its origins to the post-World War II and post-Bretton Woods era, and was not initially designed with climate action and Sustainable Development Goals (SDGs) in mind. Their continued reliance on direct lending, rather than embracing more agile indirect lending mechanisms, impedes progress in addressing contemporary challenges. Recognizing this, our efforts have centred on advocating for the realignment of these institutions to better address contemporary imperatives like climate action and SDGs.

The world is awash with financial resources, with private funds holding a staggering $ 300 trillion and sovereign wealth funds and pension funds collectively possessing nearly $ 150 trillion. However, the inherent risks faced by emerging markets significantly differ from those of developed nations. In the light of this, our advocacy for reform emphasizes the necessity for multilateral development banks to introduce innovative instruments such as blended finance, first-loss guarantees, and credit enhancements. These measures are pivotal in unlocking a tenfold increase in funding, and bridging the current gap where they mobilize a mere 0.6 cents from the private sector per dollar lent.

A critical flaw in the existing international financial architecture lies in the skewed tilt of multilateral financial institutions, particularly the IMF, in favour of developed nations. The aftermath of inflation in America, for instance, triggers rising interest rates, resulting in a flow of resources from the developing world to the developed world. This misalignment poses a fundamental challenge to fostering equitable global economic growth. Over the past two years, we have witnessed resources flowing from India to the developed world, underscoring the urgency for a recalibration.

Recognizing these systemic shortcomings, one of our key priorities has been advocating for the reform of multilateral development banks. To spearhead this transformative agenda, we established a committee led by luminaries such as Larry Summers and N. K. Singh, entrusted with crafting a comprehensive roadmap for overhauling these institutions. This commitment is rooted in the conviction that these reforms are indispensable for fostering a more equitable and resilient international financial architecture.

Accelerating Progress on SDGs

Our third priority was to galvanise an urgent re-commitment to the Sustainable Development Goals (SDGs) 2030. Compounded by the setback inflicted by the COVID-19 pandemic, only 12 per cent of the SDGs are currently on track. Recognizing the imperative to expedite progress, we spearheaded the formulation of a robust action plan, seamlessly integrated into our comprehensive G20 Leaders' Declaration. This action plan, designed for universal adoption, has garnered unanimous acceptance, and its enforcement is poised to receive proactive support from the United Nations.

The 'G20 2023 Action Plan on Accelerating Progress on the SDGs' was adopted unanimously by all G20 member-countries during the

Development Ministers' Meeting in Varanasi in June. This strategic blueprint centres on pivotal domains like digital transformation, gender equality, and sustainable transitions, aiming to expedite the attainment of SDGs on a global scale. Functioning as a dynamic multi-year framework, the plan not only intensified cooperation among various G20 work streams but also cultivated international collaborations essential for advancing SDGs worldwide. The implementation of this plan is overseen by the Development Working Group (DWG), underscoring the G20's unwavering commitment to fostering inclusive and impactful progress.

Green Development Pact for a Sustainable Future

In line with this, we directed our efforts towards advancing a Green Development Pact, cognizant of the urgent need for climate action and finance to avert global extinction. With 90 per cent of the total carbon space already claimed by the developed world, leaving scant room for developing nations, we emphasised the vital role of multilateral development institutions in restructuring and reforming. Our resounding call within the G20 for a 'greater voice and greater representation' for developing countries underscores the necessity for SDG acceleration. This strategic imperative is encapsulated in the Green Development Pact, which seeks to harmonise industrialisation without carbonisation, necessitating increased technology transfer and financial inflow. The restructuring of multilateral development institutions will act as an enabler, ensuring a more equitable global representation and a sustainable pathway for SDG acceleration.

The Green Development Pact advocates for a threefold increase in renewable energy, emphasising the Biofuel Alliance, and the development of green hydrogen. While achieving renewable electricity for 80 per cent of our energy needs is a significant milestone, addressing sectors such as refineries, fertilisers, steel, and cement poses challenges. India currently relies on imports worth $ 200 billion in fossil fuels to meet these requirements.

Our ambitious goal is to transit from an energy importer to an exporter by 2047. This necessitates leveraging the climatic advantages, particularly prevalent in the Global South, to generate renewables, harness water, produce green hydrogen, and ultimately replace fossil fuels.

This endeavour demands significant scale, size, and resource commitment. In the Green Development Pact, the G20 leaders finally acknowledged that the world needs to "rapidly and substantially scale up investment and climate finance from billions to trillions of dollars." This serves as a wakeup signal to governments, pension funds, investors, and markets, underlining the necessity to increase ambition tenfold. The acknowledgement that USD 4 trillion/year is needed for promoting clean energy technologies and developing countries need USD 5.8-5.9 trillion for their Nationally Determined Contributions provides a concrete roadmap for financial commitments.

In addition, the Green Development Pact covers a wide array of areas, including ocean conservation, reducing plastic usage, promoting circular economies, and embracing sustainable practices. Our shared priorities within this pact are dedicated to fostering robust, sustainable, and inclusive global growth.

Moreover, our attention shifted towards expediting the achievement of Sustainable Development Goals (SDGs), with the Green Development Pact standing out as a pivotal element advocating for the overhaul of multilateral institutions.

The fifth priority – technological transformation, and digital public infrastructure – gained prominence amid the climate action necessitated by COVID-19.

Technological Transformation and Digital Infrastructure

Several nations, Brazil and Kenya among them, showcased the effectiveness of digital public infrastructure amid the pandemic. In India, our achievements were notable, including the implementation of cashless and paperless COVID vaccinations and the provision of digital identities for all 1.4 billion citizens. Between 2015 and 2017, we successfully established 500 million bank accounts, integrating them with identity and mobile numbers. Today, the efficiency of our digital public infrastructure is evident as our mobile phones enable seamless fast payments.

We conduct 11 times more fast payments than America and Europe, and four times more than China. Reflecting on the past two decades, technological advancements were largely concentrated in the Western world, driven by major tech companies like Microsoft, Facebook, Google, and Apple. Similarly, China witnessed technological progress with Tencent and Alibaba. India, however, presents a distinct model, emphasising a public interest layer by providing digital identity, upon which the private sector innovates and competes. In India, Phone Pay competes with Google Pay, and Paytm competes with WhatsApp, fostering healthy competition among 40 different apps that collectively handle approximately 11 billion transactions each month.

From the foundation of these transactions, numerous start-ups like Lending Card, Pine Labs, and others have emerged, championing cashless and paperless lending. A new wave of unicorns, including Zeroda, Grow, and Upstart, focuses on wealth creation, extending the reach of the stock market to tier 2 and tier 3 rural areas. These unicorns collectively hold about 40 per cent of the stock market share through cashless and paperless wealth creation. Additionally, start-ups like Digit and Ako offer on-the-go insurance on mobile phones, streamlining a process that once took months of paperwork for individuals like myself during my early days as an officer.

The transformative possibilities brought about by these start-ups are a direct result of digital public infrastructure. Today, four billion people lack a digital identity, three billion are without a bank account, and 133 countries lack digital fast payment systems. The Global South has pioneered a model for digital public infrastructure that is low cost, open source, open API, and interoperable. This model serves as a beacon, urging other nations to adopt similar frameworks to enable direct benefit transfer to their populations.

In India, amid the challenges of COVID, we took a distinctive approach by channelling financial support directly into the bank accounts of 800 million beneficiaries, ensuring a seamless process without any leaks. Currently, we administer 700 government schemes with zero instances of financial leakage. This efficient model has significantly enhanced our productivity and serves as an exemplar for the world, showcasing a method to elevate large segments of the population above the poverty line.

Gender Equality and Empowering Women and Girls

Our final key priority centred on women-led development, a crucial aspect considering that women constitute 50 per cent of the global population. Driving growth, achieving SDGs, and transforming lives require placing women in leadership positions, empowering them, and establishing gender equality. A study by the World Economic Forum suggests that achieving gender equality may take 132 years, a timeline we cannot afford. Our commitment is to expedite this progress within the next decade. Despite opposition from some countries, we persistently advocated for the prominence of women-led development in the New Delhi Leaders' Declaration, underscoring our strong focus on women's leadership, empowerment, and gender equality. This commitment stands as a crowning achievement within the declaration.

A Presidency of Many Milestones

India's tenure as the host of the G20 went beyond the conventional realms of diplomacy, embodying a 'people's presidency.' 'Jan Bhagidari' events became a defining feature, engaging citizens from diverse backgrounds and exemplifying the power of inclusive governance.

A significant challenge faced by India was translating its 'all-of-government' approach into effective cooperative federalism across all States and Union Territories. The meticulous organisation of 220 G20 meetings across 60 cities, and engaging more than 25,000 delegates, underscored India's commitment to making the G20 platform genuinely representative and responsive to the needs of its people. Diverse initiatives, such as lake clean-ups in Manipur, urban sanitation drives in Mumbai, natural beautification in Delhi, and rapid infrastructure development in Lucknow, demonstrated this expansive and inclusive approach.

Events like the International Kite Festival in Gujarat, the Hornbill Festival in Nagaland, Model G20 sessions with schools in Bengaluru, food festivals, mini-marathons in Delhi, and various other Jan Bhagidari initiatives left a lasting impact on countless Indians, creating an opportunity to celebrate the one-ness of the world we live in. These endeavours also emphasised the importance of grounding high-level discussions in the diverse, everyday realities of the people they aimed to benefit, putting the theme of '*Vasudhaiva Kutumbakam*' (One Earth, One Family, One Future) into active practice.

Moving beyond diplomatic discussions, India's hosting of the G20 had ripple effects reaching grassroots levels. Efforts to spotlight local cultural traditions, provide employment opportunities for artisans, and contribute to a post-COVID surge in tourism showcased the presidency's impact. Cultural programs, involving over 15,000 local artists, revitalized the tourism sector, celebrating India's cultural diversity and fostering cross-cultural understanding.

Key G20 engagement groups, including Youth20, Science20, and Labour20, played a crucial role in ensuring that diverse perspectives were considered in the decision-making process. These groups facilitated meaningful dialogues, aligning the G20 agenda with the aspirations of different segments of society and incorporating expertise from civil society.

India's G20 presidency introduced several ground-breaking initiatives, redefining the dynamics of the multilateral forum. Recognising the pressing need for an overhaul in both representation and content, India played a pivotal role in expanding the G20's scope.

The establishment of the Disaster Risk Reduction group was a testament to India's commitment to addressing critical global challenges. In recent years, the frequency and intensity of disasters have escalated, threatening communities worldwide. India's proactive approach highlighted the urgency of collective action in the face of escalating climate-related events. Instances such as the devastating wildfires in Australia, severe floods in India, earthquakes in Türkiye and Morocco, and the increasing frequency of hurricanes in the Atlantic underscored the imperative for the G20 to prioritise disaster risk reduction on its agenda.

Moreover, India's leadership in acknowledging the rising threats of pandemics added another layer of significance to its G20 presidency. The COVID-19 pandemic served as a stark reminder of the interconnectedness of global health and the need for a coordinated response to mitigate future health crises.

By incorporating these critical issues into the G20 discourse, India's presidency set a precedent for a more comprehensive and proactive approach to global challenges. The emphasis on disaster risk reduction laid the foundation for a more resilient and collaborative future, reflecting India's commitment to shaping a G20 that responds effectively to the evolving needs of the world.

Additionally, the establishment of the Startup 20 Engagement Group aimed to cultivate a successful global start-up ecosystem, while the G20 Chief Scientific Advisers Roundtable (CSAR) was a pioneering initiative fostering dialogue among chief science advisers, creating collaborative frameworks for global science policy issues.

The initiation of the Startup 20 Engagement Group signified India's forward-looking approach, and recognising the critical role of start-ups in driving economic growth and fostering innovation. In a world increasingly reliant on entrepreneurial ventures, India's emphasis on cultivating a successful global start-up ecosystem underscored the need for the G20 to adapt to evolving economic landscapes.

Simultaneously, the introduction of the G20 Chief Scientific Advisers Roundtable (CSAR) marked a pioneering step towards integrating scientific expertise into policy discussions. In a rapidly changing world, where science plays a central role in addressing global challenges, CSAR served as a government-to-government initiative. By facilitating a dialogue among chief science advisers, CSAR aimed to create collaborative frameworks for tackling pressing issues related to science policy. This novel approach recognised the interdisciplinary nature of challenges and sought to leverage scientific insights for informed and effective policymaking.

These initiatives reflected India's commitment to infusing dynamism into the G20, ensuring that the forum remains relevant and responsive to the emerging needs of the global community. As technology and innovation continue to shape the future, India's G20 presidency set the stage for a more inclusive and forward-thinking approach, emphasising the importance of fostering start-ups and integrating scientific perspectives into the highest levels of global governance.

In essence, the success achieved across all the 83 paragraphs of the G20 agenda during India's presidency stands as a testament to the nation's remarkable capabilities and diplomatic prowess. This triumph was made possible through India's strategic collaboration with the Global South and emerging markets, showcasing the strength derived from unity. The bold, gutsy, and courageous approach, coupled with a willingness to take risks, became the driving force behind the achievement of consensus. A crucial element in this success was the unwavering support and leadership of Prime Minister Narendra Modi, whose stature and influence played a pivotal role in navigating the complexities of multilateral negotiations. The New Delhi Leaders' Declaration exemplifies not just India's success but also its commitment to fostering global collaboration and driving positive change for every citizen of this One Earth.

4

Inclusive Solutions for an Inclusive World

HARSH VARDHAN SHRINGLA

India's G20 presidency, under the visionary leadership of Prime Minister Shri Narendra Modi, has etched a monumental chapter in global diplomacy. The year-long journey leading up to the two-day G20 New Delhi Leaders' Summit was an exceptional demonstration of India's best practices, values and traditions. Prime Minister Modi's 'inclusive, ambitious, decisive and action-oriented' vision for India's G20 residency transformed an annual event into a mass movement and fundamentally shifted the GDP-focused view of the world to a human-centric one.

The defining feature of India's G20 presidency was its deft navigation of a volatile international landscape, arguably one of the most intricate in recent memory. By fostering an atmosphere of inclusivity, optimism and collaborative spirit in the organisation and priorities of the G20 presidency, India laid the groundwork for a strong collective will to forge a consensus.

In a remarkable trifecta, India's G20 presidency coincided with its month-long stint as president of the UN Security Council (UNSC) for December 2022, and presidency of the Shanghai Cooperation Organisation (SCO). This triple presidency wasn't a mere coincidence; in the last few years, India's global positioning has etched its name indelibly on the canvas of global diplomacy, showcasing its rising leadership stature. India has secured meaningful engagement with leading international partners, regional interlocutors and the developing world.

As a result of these diplomatic bonds, India has the distinctive honour to offer lasting and inclusive solutions and perspectives to collectively address global concerns, while acting as a bridge between developing countries and advanced economies. All this was on display during India's historic G20 presidency.

India's G20 presidency exemplified how a developing nation at the forefront of the G20 not only elevates the voices of the Global South but also empowers emerging economies to take a leading role in confronting pressing global issues. From making the G20 more inclusive by welcoming the African Union as a permanent member to tackling the climate crisis, addressing the post-COVID deceleration of the Sustainable Development Goals and navigating the complexities of the Ukraine conflict, India's chairmanship showcased the power of shared purpose. It demonstrated that India, as the G20 Chair, not only championed policies aligned with its interests but also fostered increased multilateral cooperation.

India's unique and unprecedented efforts culminated in the adoption of a substantive and far-reaching G20 New Delhi Leaders' Declaration, despite strong ideological and geopolitical differences within the group. This pivotal moment underscored the capacity of developing nations to drive positive change on the world stage.

Great Expectations

India took over the G20 presidency at a very challenging and conflicted time in the international order. The impact of the COVID-19 pandemic, exacerbated by the Ukraine conflict, evoked the threat of global recession, high inflation, and an energy and food crisis. The collateral was the slowing down of the Sustainable Development Goals (SDGs) and climate actions. Moreover, the world was more polarised than ever before.

Amidst this canvas of chaos, India was increasingly seen as a problem-solver and agenda-setter. There was a welcome expectation from India that as a large emerging economy, which has implemented innovative and inclusive measures to improve governance and the living standards of its billion-plus people, it would be able to provide solutions for the global challenges of the day. This responsibility became increasingly significant as global governance structures – that had been in place for the past eight decades – failed to prevent or resolve the crises of the past few years.

The world was turning to 'New India', one that Prime Minister Shri Narendra Modi described as *"confident in its abilities, self-reliant in its approach, and embodied inclusivity, compassion, and a commitment to global peace and cooperation."*

The priorities of India's G20 presidency were, thus, framed to shape an inclusive, sustainable global future and to share India's best practices across sectors. This ambition was set in stone by Prime Minister Modi in Bali in 2022 when he said that India's G20 presidency would be *"inclusive, ambitious, decisive and action-oriented"*. India's G20 presidency lived up to that pledge and set a precedent for a more inclusive and interconnected world order.

Inclusivity was the prime focus in India's G20 not just in terms of priorities, but also through organisation. Prime Minister Modi recognised the power of using India's G20 platform to celebrate the nation's diversity, and illustrate how this very diversity could become a unifying factor on the global stage. This mission underscored the importance of inclusivity and harmony in a world where differences often threaten to divide, reaffirming the belief that embracing diversity can bridge gaps and promote unity. It was a resounding demonstration of India's commitment to fostering a more inclusive and interconnected global community.

As part of this celebration of diversity, India organised more than 200 G20 meetings throughout the country in 60 cities, spanning every state and union territory. This comprehensive nationwide strategy allowed G20 delegates to directly encounter the diverse facets of India. Through this extensive pan-India initiative, each state had the chance to create a lasting cultural impact on the visiting delegates. These delegates, in turn, would return to their respective countries as cultural emissaries, carrying India's rich and distinctive cultural heritage with them. It was a profound exchange that transcended diplomatic formalities and fostered genuine connections among nations.

With leaders from more than 40 countries and international organisations, in addition to nine guest countries, India's G20 witnessed the highest level of engagement in the forum's 24-year history. Africa was strongly represented under India's G20 presidency with the participation of South Africa (G20 member), Comoros (President of the African Union), Nigeria, Egypt (invitee country and NEPAD Chair) and Mauritius. Furthermore, participation in the G20 under India's presidency was not confined to just G20 members or invitee countries. In a bid to enrich and broaden the base of discussions, other countries and regional and international organisations were also invited to specific G20 meetings. For instance, Norway, with an interest and expertise in the blue economy, was invited to the G20 meeting on the health of oceans.

However, Prime Minister Modi's mission of inclusivity did not end there. It was his vision to take diplomacy to the people and use a pan-India approach to make every citizen a stakeholder in India's presidency. This was made possible through the highly effective concept of 'Jan Bhagidari' or Citizen Engagement.

Over 1.5 crore citizens were actively part of the G20 process because of Jan Bhagidari events within India, and 45 lakh people across the globe. With events such as awareness rallies, selfie with monuments contests, essay and quiz competitions, workshops, marathons, walkathons, cleanliness drives, Yuva Samvaad and Model 20, the objectives of the G20 were taken to the last mile.

Spanning 37 different areas of human endeavour, including education, agriculture, trade, culture, and women's development, the Jan Bhagidari initiative connected global ideals to everyday lives. Through close collaboration between the G20 Secretariat, State governments and Union Territories, and Line Ministries, India's G20 became a 'People's 20'.

The University Connect programme was also a resounding success, with the enthusiastic participation of students and faculty from 101 universities. Under the rubric of this program, higher education institutions across the country organised special programs disseminating information about G20 and India's role in its year-long presidency. This program touched more than 100,000 students in schools, colleges and universities.

The result of this nation-wide participation was the unprecedented popularity and celebration of India's G20. Crafted from the collective ingenuity of thousands of Indians, the G20 logo became a ubiquitous symbol of national pride. The logo was inspired by the colours of India's national flag – saffron, white, green, and blue, and blends the Earth with the lotus, India's national flower symbolising growth amid challenges. The Earth embodies India's eco-conscious approach, harmonising with nature and beneath the G20 emblem is 'Bharat' in the Devanagari script.

The theme of India's G20 presidency – 'Vasudhaiva Kutumbakam' or 'One Earth One Family One Future' – was drawn from the ancient Sanskrit text of the *Maha Upanishad*. Essentially, the theme affirms the value of all life – human, animal, plant, and micro-organism – and their interconnectedness on planet Earth and in the wider universe. It conveys a powerful message of India's G20 presidency, which is of striving for just and equitable growth for all in the world, as we navigate through these turbulent times in a sustainable, holistic, responsible, and inclusive manner. They represent a uniquely Indian approach to our G20 presidency, of living in harmony with the surrounding ecosystem.

Blending Domestic and Global

India's inclusive approach followed under the G20 presidency is an extension of its existing domestic approach to development and progress, which specifically focuses on engaging all sections of society, particularly the weaker sections. Take the digital public infrastructure, for instance. It has enabled the government to deliver the benefits of development directly to citizens in all parts of the country and has achieved this goal in a transparent, smooth, and corruption-free manner.

The Direct Benefit Transfer Scheme was implemented through the Digital Public Infrastructure, along with the 'Jan Dhan Aadhaar' trinity of identity cards, affordable internet telephony rates and 'banking the unbankable.' Through this scheme, 480 million previously 'un-banked' Indian citizens now hold bank accounts and directly receive government benefits from programmes such as the National Rural Landless Employment Guarantee scheme or the Pradhan Mantri Garib Kalyan package.

The Pradhan Mantri Jan Dhan Yojana benefits women immensely as 56 per cent of the Jan Dhan account holders are women with 67 per cent of these accounts based in rural and semi-urban areas. This fact underlines the quintessentially inclusive character of India's development programme.

It is not surprising therefore that 'women-led development' is a major priority of India's G20 presidency.

In a similar vein, the approach towards public health has also been inclusive and impactful. Through the COWIN platform, over 2 billion vaccines have been administered to our citizens. Additionally, the 'Ayushman Bharat' scheme, the world's largest publicly-funded health insurance scheme, has touched the lives of over 500 million citizens.

Another crucial area of focus has been sanitation and availability of drinking water with more than 110 million sanitation facilities created across the country. In addition, about 110 million rural households out of 150 million have also been provided with access to drinking water at their homes. The 'Har Ghar Jal' initiative aims at ensuring that every household has access to water. These are just some examples of India's commitment towards inclusive development which aims at involving all its citizens, especially those from the weaker sections of the society.

Global Public Good

The challenge of inclusivity lies in making sure that every single citizen in a country is provided with the basic necessities of life while ensuring that there is enough social security support for them, and India has consistently made massive strides in this aspect. Working for the global public good has been an important objective of India's foreign policy as was evident during the COVID-19 pandemic. India shared medicines like hydroxychloroquine with over 190 countries in the world while also sharing the 'Made in India' vaccines with over 150 countries through the 'Vaccine Maitri' programme. In the past decade or so, India's development assistance quantum has doubled and lines of credit have expanded from $ 14 billion to almost $ 30 billion. Furthermore, within the Indo-Pacific region, India, along with some of its partners, is a first responder in extending humanitarian action and disaster relief.

A key priority of India's G20 presidency was to create a more inclusive world that reflected the realities of the 21st century, where the voice of the Global South would no longer be overlooked. The greatest achievement in this regard was the acceptance of India's proposal to welcome the African

Union as a permanent member at the G20. The African Union's membership in the G20 is an opportunity to promote sustainable development in Africa. Now, as a permanent member, it can work with other G20 members to mobilise resources and expertise to support Africa's development priorities including investments in infrastructure, education, and healthcare.

Furthermore, the G20 nations reaffirmed that today's challenges are inter-connected and can only be addressed through reinvigorated multilateralism, reforms and international cooperation. G20 nations agreed that a more inclusive and reinvigorated multilateralism, and reform aimed at implementing the 2030 agenda is essential.

Member-nations thus agreed that the 21st century requires an international development finance system that is fit for this purpose, including for the scale of need and depth of the shocks facing developing countries.

The G20 committed to pursue ambitious efforts to evolve multilateral development banks to address the global challenges of the 21st century with a focus on addressing the development needs of low- and middle-income countries. In this regard, the G20 Roadmap for Implementing the Recommendations of the G20 Independent Review of MDBs Capital Adequacy Frameworks (CAFs) was welcomed.

Debt resolution under the common framework, and also beyond the common framework, was another major outcome of India's G20 presidency for the inclusive development of the Global South. The Global Sovereign Debt roundtable was also launched in this regard. Co-chaired by the IMF, the World Bank, and also the G20 presidency, this will enhance the conversation among the various stakeholders and address current shortcomings in the debt restructuring process.

India's proposal to create 'One Future Alliance' was welcomed, which is a voluntary initiative aimed at building capacity, and providing technical assistance and adequate funding support for implementing digital public infrastructure in low and middle income countries.

The Millets and Other Ancient Grains International Research Initiative (MAHARISHI), launched under G20 India in the International Year of

Millets, is another significant initiative that has the potential to benefit the Global South in a number of ways.

The G20 agreed that climate finance is not only essential for addressing climate change, but is also a key driver of inclusive and sustainable growth in the Global South. Under India's presidency, developed countries in the G20 reaffirmed their commitment to the goal of jointly mobilising $ 100 billion climate finance per year annually by 2025 to address the needs of developing countries, with the contributors expected to meet this goal for the first time in 2023. This is especially significant given the potential of climate finance to create new jobs and opportunities in the Global South, while also promoting sustainable development. This is an investment in our collective future.

Through its unique approach, India's presidency has not only left an indelible mark on the G20 but has also set a remarkable precedent that our brethren of the Global South, Brazil and South Africa, will take forward. Our democratic ethos and unwavering commitment to ambitious outcomes have forged a path towards a new, inclusive and sustainable global order.

By firmly believing in inclusivity and taking everyone on board the path to growth and prosperity, India has shown what it means to lead by example. At a time when multiple crises of a global magnitude affect us all, the importance of keeping 'Vasudhaiva Kutumbakam's' sentiment alive has never been more critical.

India's Moment:
Forging a Value-based Future

SUJAN R. CHINOY

On 1 December 2022, India officially took over the presidency of G20. The build-up towards it was palpable. On 8 November 2022, PM Narendra Modi launched the logo, website and theme for India's presidency. 'Vasudhaiva Kutumbakam' was the quintessence of India's slogan for the G20, eloquently captured by the theme 'One Earth, One Family, One Future'. Apart from the colours of the national flag, the logo depicted a lotus flower with seven petals on which symbolically rests the Earth, its oceans and the seven continents signalling a pro-planet approach. Through this holistic, culturally evocative logo, India aspired to transcend geographical and other limitations and embrace the whole world in its endeavour to bring peace, development and prosperity for all.

Rise of the Global South

India's G20 presidency coincided with its rising global stature and a high economic growth rate. Ever since the G20 was re-launched as an annual apex level summit in the aftermath of the 2008 global financial and economic crises, developing countries have chaired it only on four occasions – Mexico in 2012, China in 2016, Argentina in 2018 and, Indonesia in 2022. The Indian presidency marked the fifth such occasion. Preceded by Indonesia, India passed the baton of the G20 to Brazil which, in turn, will be followed by South Africa in 2025.

India's commitment to advancing high-impact South-South cooperation is well acknowledged. Even at the height of the COVID-19 pandemic, India provided 250 million vaccine doses to 101 countries, besides other medical assistance. The G20 presidency provided India with yet another opportunity to emerge as a voice of the Global South. In January 2023, Prime Minister Narendra Modi gave impetus to the year-long exercise of building consensus by hosting the first virtual Voice of the Global South Summit. He also aptly concluded the presidency by hosting the second such virtual summit in November 2023. Inspired by the philosophy of 'Vasudhaiva Kutumbakam', India proposed and steered the inclusion of the African Union (AU) into the G20 at the New Delhi Summit, based on its strong advocacy of 'leaving none behind'. This momentous development, which makes the G20 structure more representative, highlights India's role as a true friend and representative of the Global South.

Relevance of G20

India's G20 presidency was not without its challenges. The world was already divided after the war in Ukraine broke out, leaving developing countries to suffer the most from shortages of food, fuel, fertilisers and finance. The UN-led multilateral framework proved ineffective in addressing the key challenges before the international community, whether they were peace and security, climate change or economic recovery in the post-pandemic period. Across Asia, Africa, Latin America and vulnerable island-nations, the overwhelming preoccupations revolved around trade and fiscal issues, including the urgent need for adequate finance and technology to effect just and equitable green transitions.

The G20 presidency offered India a platform to articulate a value-based future for humanity based on an alternative and inclusive vision. Today, the UN, created at the end of the Second World War, is mired in major power contestation involving the permanent members of the Security Council. They have been unable to work together as they should in accordance with the Charter of the UN. Their differences have threatened to spill over into the functioning of other global dialogue platforms such as the G20, whose mandate pivots around the economic, financial and developmental issues, not political and military issues.

Efforts to reform multilateral institutions such as the Security Council have come to nought because of the vested interests of the permanent members to preserve a monopoly over power. The impasse over UN reforms and the glacial pace of change at multilateral institutions such as the World Bank and the IMF gave India's G20 presidency a new sense of urgency.

Under India's leadership, the G20 grouping became the key international platform of debate and discourse as well as reform and reconciliation. Building consensus was difficult in the hundreds of meetings and, for a while, it appeared that forging a Delhi Declaration would prove elusive. Yet, when it came to the finishing line, India managed to ensure that all 83 paragraphs of the G20 New Delhi Leaders' Declaration were adopted by consensus.

Continuity and Change

India's stewardship of the G20 was defined by continuity and change. Differences over energy diversification and the emerging challenges in trade and technology cried out for reconciliation. Flagging economic growth in major economies around the world threatened the global economic outlook. Against this backdrop, policy coherence in macroeconomics and trade became an imperative.

Food security emerged as one of the key challenges before the developing nations. India's proposal to observe 2023 as the International Year of Millets was approved by the Food and Agriculture Organization (FAO) and endorsed by the UNGA at its 75th session in March 2021. As one of the world's largest producers of millets, India introduced the Millet International Initiative for Research and Awareness (MIIRA) during its G20 presidency.

India's commitment to digital transformation and to accessible and inclusive digital public architecture is well-known. India's success with the Unified Payments Interface (UPI), the Direct Benefits Transfer and Aadhaar authentication in various welfare schemes is of growing relevance to the developing world. It found natural resonance in the documents that emerged during India's G20 presidency. It added to the earlier success that India had achieved with the digital delivery of vaccines via the Co-WIN platform to its large population.

India has endeavoured to develop consensus on open source, open Application Programming Interface (API) and an interoperable framework for public digital platforms in which the private sector can freely innovate during its presidency. Its relevance to the achievement of the UN's 2030 Agenda on Sustainable Development cannot be over-estimated. Climate change remains an abiding theme. At COP26 in Glasgow, Modi proposed Mission LiFE, which places individual behaviour at the heart of the global climate action narrative. The Mission intends to establish and nurture a global network of individuals known as 'Pro-Planet People' (P3), committed to adopting and promoting environment-friendly lifestyles.

Now codified as the G20 High Level Principles on Lifestyles for Sustainable Development, this mission is a profound idea that links the tiniest of irresponsible human actions to damage wrought upon Nature. On its part, India is the only G20 country to have achieved its Paris Agreement goals well before the stipulated target of 2030.

The urgency to resolve the matter of funding for climate change mitigation, adaptation and transition in the next few years is a common thread that ran through the COP28 as well as the G20 deliberations. A balance must be struck between growth and green energy. Developing countries will have to protect their basic position of CBDR (Common But Differentiated Responsibilities) from being eroded by those that have already developed, but now seek to put the burden of future growth in the Global South on developing countries without accepting their historical role in creating the problem of climate change.

The challenge of climate change can be met in a time-bound manner only if the world acts in unison. As PM Modi said, the achievement of inclusive energy transition requires affordable sources of finance and technological assistance. The G20 presidency provided India an opportunity to give a fresh impetus to several of its initiatives for clean energy partnerships and green transitions, especially solar, wind and hydrogen. It also provided a platform to give a fillip to the idea of 'One Sun, One World, One Grid (OSOWOG)', first mooted by PM Modi at the International Solar Alliance (ISA) in 2018.

Clean energy and achievement of the Sustainable Development Goals

(SDGs) can be mutually reinforcing. Green Hydrogen (GH2) can credibly replace fossil fuels on a large industrial scale, including in hard-to-abate sectors such as refineries, fertilisers, transport and cement. India has the scale and capacity to set a shining example of rapid and decarbonised economic growth to help realise the G20's global net zero ambitions. Another example is the launch of the Global Biofuel Alliance at the G20 Summit in 2023 with the aim of boosting supply and demand for bio fuels. PM Modi had earlier stated during the G20 Leaders' Summit that "through the Global Biofuel Alliance launched in New Delhi, we are reducing carbon as well as promoting the development of alternative fuels".

A Better Future

The author was fortunate to Chair the Think20 engagement group, the 'Ideas Bank' of the G20. It comprised scholars, academicians and experts from around the world who contributed to various sessions throughout the year, discussing matters of critical importance such as LiFE, fiscal policies, reform of multilateralism and more. At the concluding Summit of the Think20 in Mysuru, it was agreed that many of the research themes were worthy of continuation by successive presidencies. Many of the rich ideas and analyses are contained in the hundreds of policy briefs published by the Think20 Secretariat, reflecting the distilled wisdom of experts from institutions around the world.

G20 may not be perfect in providing a panacea for all the major global challenges. It is, nevertheless, a powerful, representative forum with a progressive and resilient structure. India's G20 presidency has infused a new hope through a value-based leadership, reconciled contradictions and enabled the global community to forge creative solutions to traditional problems.

G20 India: A Diplomatic and Organisational Feat

MUKTESH PARDESHI

On watching the elegant G20 tableau float past at the Republic Day Parade on 26 January 2024, India's External Affairs Minister Dr. S. Jaishankar proudly exclaimed in his 'X' post, "What an year it was!" Indeed 2023 was an incredible year for India to emerge as a prime mover of decisive diplomacy and an impeccable host for the premier forum for international economic cooperation – the Group of 20. A successful G20 presidency has undoubtedly put the stamp on India's organisational excellence and diplomatic heft.

Earlier, a week after the conclusion of the New Delhi G20 Summit (9-10 September 2023), Prime Minister Shri Narendra Modi, addressing a special session of Parliament on 18 September, had said that "the success of the G20 is the success of 1.4 billion citizens of India…not the success of any individual or party. India's federal structure, its diversity, and its hosting of over 200 meetings in more than 60 locations, each with its own unique flavour, has been done magnificently by different state governments. This impact has been felt on the global stage…and enhances the glory of the nation."

The above statement so eloquently captures India's visionary organisational approach to its year-long presidency, which has widely been recognised as a great success on all counts. The term, which began on 1 December 2022, had completed ten months of its substantive work by the time the leaders gathered for the 18th G20 Summit in India's capital. Here, in an unprecedented and outcome-oriented move, Prime Minister Modi announced that the leaders would again virtually convene towards the end of November 2023 to take stock of the progress made on the New Delhi Summit recommendations. The outcomes of the 2nd Voice of Global South Summit held on 17 November also fed into the Virtual Summit deliberations on 22 November. Thereafter, Brazil officially took over on 1 December 2023. India continues to be a part of the G20 Troika, together with Brazil and South Africa and would continue to take forward the outcomes achieved during its presidency, as well as the shared priorities of the Global South.

There has been a great deal of popular support for the country's diplomatic efforts. Like the moment of the Chandrayaan-3 landing in the last week of August 2023, the G20 presidency has been a high point for India's global leadership, public policy-making and showcasing India to the world; it has now become a part of the Indian lexicon.

To shed light on the multifaceted, human-centric approach underpinning India's G20 presidency, we can identify seven key 'petals' characterising both its substantive and organisational legacy:

A Visionary Approach: Inclusiveness

The making of India's presidency has been inspired by an inclusive vision of 'Taking G20 to the Last Mile, Leaving None Behind'. Speaking at the Bali Summit 2022, Prime Minister Narendra Modi articulated that India assumed leadership of this intergovernmental forum during a period marked by concurrent challenges of geopolitical tensions, economic deceleration, surging food and energy costs, and the enduring repercussions of the pandemic. He pledged that India's stewardship would be 'inclusive, ambitious, decisive, and action-oriented', and that "together, we [would] make the G20 a catalyst for global change". This inclusive approach unfolded as we steered the presidency by embracing an agenda with human-centric progress at its core.

An Effective Organisational Plan

The absence of a permanent secretariat or dedicated staff within the G20 framework places the onus to establish a robust support system on the presidency.

Our presidency had been in the making for some time. At the 2018 G20 Summit in Argentina, India had sought a swap with Italy so that it could be president of the grouping during the 75th anniversary of its Independence in 2022. This did not go through. Later, Indonesia proposed a swap with India due to the fact that it would be chairing the Association of Southeast Asian Nations (ASEAN) in 2023. This rotational arrangement was mutually agreed on. Therefore, the actual preparations for India's presidency began in right earnest when it joined the 'troika' on 1 December 2021, along with Italy as past president and Indonesia as incoming president.

In a major development, on 15 February 2022, the Union Cabinet approved the setting up of a G20 secretariat and its reporting structures for the implementation of overall policy decisions and arrangements needed for steering India's presidency until February 2024. Subsequently, the secretariat swiftly assumed operational status, shouldering responsibilities related to substantive matters, technical intricacies, media management, security protocols, and overall organisational plans. It was guided by an apex committee headed by the Prime Minister, and comprised the Finance Minister, Home Minister, External Affairs Minister, and the G20 Sherpa to provide overall guidance to the presidency.

Notably, the New Delhi Summit marked Prime Minister Modi's 10th participation in a G20 Summit. As a host leader, he had tasked the secretariat to develop an organisational plan to give a "full experience of India's amazing diversity, inclusive traditions, and cultural richness" to the visiting guests. This could only have been possible by adopting a 'whole-of-country approach', in which Central Government Ministries, States and Union Territories, and local bodies become stakeholders. This approach emerged as India's guiding mantra.

Unifying Principles: Logo and Theme

India's G20 logo was unveiled by Prime Minister Modi on 8 November

2022. It drew inspiration from the vivid hues of India's national flag – saffron, white, green, and blue. Within this logo, a harmonious juxtaposition emerges, as it interweaves the image of Planet Earth with the lotus, India's national flower, symbolising growth amidst challenges. The Earth symbolises India's deeply-rooted pro-planet ethos, reflecting a life in perfect alignment with the natural world. Below the G20 logo is 'Bharat' written in the Devanagari script. The logo drew upon elements contained in over 2,000 different entries received in May 2022 during an open competition for the design on the MyGov portal.

The theme of India's G20 presidency – *'Vasudhaiva Kutumbakam'* or 'One Earth, One Family, One Future' – is drawn from the ancient Sanskrit text of the *Maha Upanishad*. Essentially, it affirms the value of all life – human, animal, and plant – and its interconnectedness in the wider universe. During the conceptualisation of this theme, it became evident that India was championing a philosophy that emphasises the value of all living beings, the bonds that unite us, and our collective destiny.

The logo and the theme together conveyed a powerful message of India's G20 presidency, which is of striving for a just and equitable growth as we navigate through turbulent times in a sustainable, holistic, responsible, and inclusive manner. India committed to take all along; its pledge has been to ensure that no one is left behind, thus encapsulating the essence of 'G20 for all.'

Advancing the G20 Agenda

India has been an active participant in the G20 ever since it was founded in 1999 as an informal forum for the finance ministers and central bank governors of the most important industrialised and developing economies. India hosted a meeting of G20 finance ministers and central bank governors in 2002.

The presidency is responsible for bringing together the G20 agenda in consultation with other members, especially the 'troika', in response to developments in the global economy. During India's presidency, the members of the 'troika' have been Indonesia, India and Brazil, all dynamic emerging economies.

India formally announced the date, the list of special invitee countries and organisations, and the major thematic priorities on 13 September 2022. In addition to the core member-countries, encompassing 19 nations and the European Union, each G20 presidency has invited guest countries and international organisations (IOs) to participate in the meetings and Summit. India invited Bangladesh, Egypt, Mauritius, the Netherlands, Nigeria, Oman, Singapore, Spain and the UAE as guest countries. For Guest IOs, it invited ISA, CDRI and ADB in addition to the regular IOs (UN, IMF, WB, WHO, WTO, ILO, FSB and OECD) and Chairs of Regional Organisations (AU, AUDA-NEPAD and ASEAN). Therefore, New Delhi saw the participation of nine invitee countries and 14 IOs, apart from the regular members.

The September announcement also mentioned that whilst our G20 priorities were in the process of being firmed up, ongoing conversations indicated that the agenda will revolve around inclusive, equitable and sustainable growth; LiFE (Lifestyle For Environment); women's empowerment; digital public infrastructure and tech-enabled development in areas ranging from health, agriculture and education to commerce, skill-mapping, culture and tourism; climate financing; circular economy; global food and energy security; green hydrogen; disaster risk reduction and resilience; developmental cooperation; fight against economic crime; and multilateral reforms.

Several noteworthy additions were also made to the agenda by the Indian presidency. These include the establishment of a new working group focused on disaster risk reduction, the introduction of a new startup20 engagement group, and the implementation of two distinct Initiatives: a roundtable of chief scientific advisors and a conference on cyber security. Our ambitious agenda comprised a comprehensive array of 37 work streams and subject areas, encompassing vital domains such as trade, climate change, sustainable development, health, agriculture, energy, environment, climate change, and anti-corruption, among others. India ensured that global attention was directed to broader developmental goals.

Giving Voice to the Global South

When India assumed the presidency in December 2022, it was acutely conscious that most of the Global South would not have a direct seat at the G20 table. Therefore, a strategic decision was made to convene the 'Voice of the Global South Summit' in January 2023. India heard from 125 nations directly about their challenges and priorities and amplifying these voices took its presidency to a higher plane.

Moreover, the year saw the highest participation from Africa at the New Delhi Summit: South Africa (the only African member-country till now), Mauritius, Egypt, Nigeria, African Union Chair (Comoros), and the African Union Development Agency-New Partnership for Africa's Development (AUDA-NEPAD). After seven years of advocating for full membership, the support for a permanent membership for the African Union, which till now was an invitee international organisation, gained momentum under India's leadership. In his opening remarks at the inaugural session of the summit on 9 September, 2024, Prime Minister Modi announced the admission of the 55-nation regional bloc (the second after the 27-member European Union) as a full member of the grouping.

Africa continues to disproportionately suffer from major global challenges and crises like climate change, food and energy insecurity, health disparity, inequality, and debt distress. Therefore, the G20 membership is an important complement to the Union's existing multilateral and bilateral strategic partnerships and this move has been hugely welcomed for giving the continent an important voice on key global issues.

Narrating the India Story

Over 200-plus meetings across India provided unique opportunities to present and share the India story with the global community, be it its diversity, culture, democracy, development and technological transformation. More than 60,000 delegates were hosted across the length and breadth of India – from Lakshadweep and the Andaman & Nicobar Islands in the south to Jammu & Kashmir in the north, Gujarat and Diu in the west to Assam and Arunachal Pradesh in the east.

At the newly-built summit venue, Bharat Mandapam, several thematic exhibits were installed to promote India's soft power: 'Bharat: Mother of Democracy', which highlighted that "taking the consent of the people in governance has been part of life since earliest recorded history". It also included a Digital India Experience Zone and Crafts Bazaar, which showcased and sold handicrafts products from different parts of India with a special focus on 'One District One Product' (ODOP), Geographical Indication (GI) tagged items and products crafted by women and tribal artisans. Delegates also enjoyed special live demonstrations by master craftsmen, enhancing the immersive experience.

People's G20

The 2023 presidency, which came to India for the first time, was more than just a multilateral diplomatic endeavour; it evolved into a year-long national undertaking and celebration, involving the entire Central Government, all 36 States and Union Territories, Parliament, businesses, hospitality industry, academia, professionals, scientists, cultural groups, media, and most notably, the youth.

In the annals of independent India's history, there has never been an event of such magnitude and scope carried out over an entire year, touching every corner of the nation. We embraced a distinctive approach, pioneered by Prime Minister Modi himself in his *Mann Ki Baat* radio address (November 2022), emphasising the infusion of *Jan Bhagidari* (People's Participation) into our endeavours. Aligning with this vision, we achieved an unparalleled geographical reach for G20 meetings, with 230 meetings scheduled across 60 different locations – a remarkable feat under any G20 presidency. In the history of the G20 grouping, the largest footprint of meetings has been achieved by India. In comparison, Indonesia conducted its 2022 meetings in 25 cities, Italy in 13 in 2021, Japan in nine in 2019, and Argentina in 11 in 2018. China and Germany held their gatherings in 12 and seven cities, respectively, in 2016 and 2017.

India' success in engaging its citizenry as active participants in the global discourse stands as a testament to its commitment to inclusivity. India's presidency transcended traditional diplomatic boundaries.

Thus, we witnessed throughout the year a profound and palpable sense of national pride amongst people apropos India's successful G20 presidency and its pivotal role in projecting India onto the global stage. For India, the year of leadership also marked the beginning of *Amritkaal,* the 25-year period leading up to the centenary of its independence in 2047, towards a prosperous, inclusive and *Viksit Bharat* (developed India). In this context, our G20 leadership has created an enduring legacy, both globally as well as domestically, by bolstering our infrastructure, capacity and image in physical, intellectual, and organisational domains, showcasing India's potential to the world, and shaping a positive global narrative that will resonate for years to come.

Shared Priorities: From Indian G20 Presidency to Italian G7 Presidency

His Excellency Vincenzo de Luca

As new strategic partners (since March 2023), Italy and India have not only a bilateral agenda in common, but also an increasingly shared responsibility for leadership and coordination in international forums. It is but natural that there is a connection in terms of objectives and outcomes between India's G20 presidency in 2023, and the current Italian G7 presidency (2024).

Saving Multilateralism

In a challenging international scenario with overlapping conflicts, Italy is well aware of the legacy emanating from the New Delhi Declaration, which was adopted during the G20 summit under India's presidency (9 September 2023). Indian diplomacy succeeded in obtaining a joint declaration that was far from given in the context of tremendous international tensions caused by the war in Ukraine and the competition between the USA and China. India demonstrated its negotiating skills and presented itself as a leader of the Global South, with the ambition to be a bridge between the heterogeneous bloc that is the Global South and the West. At the same time, India has voiced widespread demands for the reform of the multilateral system and is paying more and more attention not only to Asia but also to Africa, where it intersects the Italian government's priorities. By contributing to the adoption of the G20 joint declarations – both in Bali (2022) and in New Delhi (2023), India has made a tremendous effort to save multilateralism from failure, in line with the Italian vision of a rule-based order with effective multilateral forums.

Rule-based Order

During its G7 presidency in 2024, Italy will focus on reducing systemic risks, reaffirming a rule-based order based on the respect for the UN Charter. Under the Italian presidency, the G7 will seek inclusiveness and broad international support as much as possible, avoiding a further polarization of the international agenda. Fragmentation between the G7 and the Global South as well as duplication must be reduced in order to overcome the logic of globalization and restructure and diversify supply chains in the direction of greater security and resilience. In this sense, the Italian presidency of the G7 continues the overarching message of the Indian G20 presidency: if "this is not a time of war", then an apparent antagonism between 'the West' and 'the Rest' has to be avoided.

Lotus and Olive Tree

The Italian presidency's logo, an olive tree, indicates the importance of 'connective power' in a world in conflict: as the situation in the Red Sea shows' without security, stability and peace, global public goods such as prosperity, development and sustainability are at risk for everyone, developed and developing countries alike. Even when it comes to symbolism, it is hard not to see the similarity of the Italian olive tree with the Indian lotus flower under the motto 'Vasudhaiva Kutumbakam' – One Earth, One Family, One Future of the G20 presidency.

Without ignoring major current conflicts such as those in Gaza and Ukraine, the stability in the Indo-Pacific will also be at the centre of the G7 discussions: corridors such as the India-Mediterranean-East-Europe-Economic Corridor (IMEC) are a priority for global balances and critical for the trade routes to the Mediterranean and freedom of navigation. A particular topic of interest will be economic coercion and the response to it, which will have to balance de-risking with sound economic relations.

Focus on Africa

The G7 presidency is also an opportunity for Italy to put Africa at the centre of the agenda, as happened during the Indian G20 presidency when the African Union became – with Italy's support – a full member of the G20 format. Italy intends to renew its commitment to work together with the countries of the African continent, in a spirit of mutual respect and on an equal footing, including in the context of the G7 'Partnership for Africa' and in the implementation of the Sustainable Development Goals. With its G7 presidency, Italy will promote a paradigm shift in relation with African partners, adopting an inclusive approach based on three pillars: listen-respect-build together. This is also the vision of the Mattei Plan for Africa. Investing in energy transition and the development of new technologies will be fundamental to ensure that Africa fully realizes its potential as a 'renewable energy superpower', in the words of UN Secretary-General Antonio Guterres. In this context, Italy will also address the development-migration nexus, tackling the root causes of irregular migration and promoting sustainable growth on the continent.

Global Issues

Major transnational issues, such as Artificial Intelligence, will also be at the centre of the Italian presidency. Artificial Intelligence opens up enormous opportunities for humanity but also poses significant risks, raising the question of global governance of this phenomenon so that an approach centred on respect for human dignity prevails. Equally relevant are the possible consequences of Artificial Intelligence on international relations, especially in the geo-strategic sphere, and in particular, the new capabilities it generates at the level of knowledge, intrusion and destabilisation ('weaponisation'). The need to steer the digital transition towards modes compatible with the democratic values of an open society also remains crucial. This awareness of technological development is also a topic that reconnects the Italian G7 presidency with India's G20 presidency, which put the Digital Public Infrastructure (DPI) at its core. Moreover, during its G20 presidency, India hosted the first G20 Ministerial Conference on Crime and Security in the Age of NFTs, AI and the Metaverse (13-14 July 2023).

Finally, the G7 led by Italy in 2024 will deal with energy transition and climate change. These are issues that, together with economic security and food security, and more generally the achievement of the Sustainable Development Goals, require the maximum commitment of the entire international community. This is also true in the light of the COP28 outcomes which represent a good compromise in the direction of a 'transition away from fossil fuels' and with regard to the confirmation of the 'Loss and Damage'. To this end, the G7 will undertake work with emerging countries or belonging to other ad hoc groups (which represent about two-thirds of the members of the United Nations), keeping channels of dialogue open at all times and promoting, where possible, joint actions with global partners.

Cooperation between the G7 and the G20 will be crucial and strategic in this respect. In the exercise of its G7 presidency, Italy will seek spaces for active, 'agenda-driven' cooperation with the Brazilian G20 presidency, drawing inspiration from previous presidencies, including India's.

8

Shared Legacy: Ending Poverty and Reforming Global Governance

HIS EXCELLENCY KENNETH FELIX HACZYNSKI DA NOBREGA

India's G20 presidency produced outstanding results and achieved a lot against a complex geopolitical background. Among them, I would like to single out three, which hold special significance for the future of the grouping and for the goals to be achieved in the short term during Brazil's G20 presidency. They include the mainstreaming of the interests and challenges faced by the countries of the Global South; the issuance of a joint statement by the G20 leaders which encompassed the most complex issues of the day, including the war in Ukraine, and last but not the least, the inclusion of the African Union as a permanent G20 member which epitomized the aspirations of the Global South as a whole.

Continuity and Consensus

The Brazilian presidency will be, to a considerable extent, one of continuity. Brazil is the third in a sequence of four developing countries chairing the grouping, following in the footsteps of Indonesia in 2022 and India in 2023. Brazil's G20 presidency will be followed by South Africa's in 2025. There is continuity in the drive to consolidate the interests and challenges of developing countries in the grouping's agenda, and in the commitment to the tireless pursuit of consensus and inclusiveness under the rubric of promoting peace and sustainable development for all humanity.

For Brazil, the G20 remains the best-placed global forum to engender the solutions the world needs for the many challenges on the horizon. Its diverse membership can be an asset rather than a hindrance, as the solutions needed will only emerge from enhanced dialogue, one open to many different voices. The G20 is not, however, a substitute for multilateral organizations. It does not have the tools or the membership to replace established multilateral fora. The United Nations is, and should remain, at the centre of global governance.

Global Challenges

Brazil sees the G20's role as a crucial conduit to muster political will towards concrete changes, especially in times of multiple and cascading world crises that seem to bounce off each other, and so require stronger international cooperation to be overcome. These crises reach far and wide like persistent hunger, poverty and inequality; armed conflicts and their catastrophic humanitarian consequences; the widespread setbacks in living standards; inflation and debt vulnerabilities; high volatility in food and energy prices and a climate crisis that is no longer a distant threat but rather a grim reality for far too many. These challenges are all amplified by both old and new geopolitical tensions. While they touch us all, they do not do so equally or uniformly. Developing countries and their populations are more likely to bear the brunt of them. The distributional effects of all these crises, both between countries as well as within themselves, should not be diminished.

According to President Lula, if we had to summarize the current global challenges in a single word, it would be inequality. Inequality is the root cause of the many crises we face today and is a major contributing factor to their aggravation. For this reason, Brazil has been endeavouring to mainstream the challenge of inequality reduction in all its dimensions. This effort is also present in this G20 agenda. We must tackle problems that range from geopolitical conflicts to hunger and malnutrition, from climate change to the risks of new pandemics, from sticky inflation to a rise in poverty levels.

Brazil's Three Priorities

It is in this spirit that Brazil proposes three priorities for its G20 presidency under the banner of 'Building a Just World and a Sustainable Planet'. These focus on social inclusion and the fight against hunger and poverty; energy transitions and the promotion of sustainable development in its economic, social, and environmental dimensions; and reform of global governance institutions. The implementation of these priorities has been fostered by promoting greater integration between the financial and political tracks and work streams within the group striving for what is essentially a result-oriented presidency, connecting political ideas to their economic viability and to the availability of resources.

To address the first priority, the Brazilian presidency has created the Global Alliance against Hunger and Poverty. As we know, the progress towards achieving the 2030 agenda of SDG 1 and 2 has not only stalled but also suffered serious setbacks since the COVID-19 pandemic. According to the United Nations Food and Agriculture Organization (FAO), around 735 million individuals currently face hunger and some 4 billion people face moderate to severe food insecurity. Let us remember that of these, 150 million are children under the age of five. To help reverse this situation, the alliance will take concrete steps to mainstream a set of established domestic public policy instruments that have proven successful in developing countries, such as targeted cash transfers, school meal programs, support for family farming, single registry systems for low-income persons and families and social security mechanisms. These policies, when successful, have proved to have a mutually reinforcing link with economic growth.

The proposed alliance will be structured on the three pillars of national commitment, financial availability and technical support. Their scope is comprehensive and adaptable to specific needs so that countries facing hunger can commit to adopting those public policies that have already proved successful. They will have access to technical cooperation and financial funds, including the possibility of debt swaps. Rich countries and those with emerging economies can provide either financial support or technical cooperation to help in the implementation of successful hunger-fighting policies. South-to-South cooperation will play an important role in this global alliance as many countries of the Global South have managed to overcome hunger in the last decades: Brazil and India are among them.

Combating Hunger and Poverty

A global alliance against hunger and poverty would be open to the participation of all countries and not only of G20 members. To ensure efficiency and cohesion, the G20 is joining efforts with United Nations organisations such as the FAO, International Labour Organization (ILO) and the World Food Programme (WFP). Work has also been carried out with the World Bank and other multilateral development banks. President Lula has actively been conveying this message of the importance of the participation of all countries in the task force. The issue was recently addressed with African leaders during the summit of the African Union held in Addis Ababa.

The alliance's governance will rely on a lean steering committee, supported by a small secretariat assembled in partnership with selected international organisations. It is not the intention to establish new funds or to create new organisations, but rather to make better use of existing ones through a new and more comprehensive approach.

Climate Change

A second task force on 'Global Mobilization to Address Climate Change' will also bring together the Sherpa and the Finance tracks and explore avenues such as the role of national sustainability transformation plans in economy-wide platforms and a renewed agenda for the engagement of the financial sector in climate action. There cannot be meaningful results in the fight against climate change without sufficient timely and easily accessible financial resources. To deliver unprecedented investments that are required to match the needs, the transitions in most countries, especially in developing ones, require the transformation of the financial system, its structures and processes. One needs to engage governments, central banks, financial regulators, commercial and development banks, international financial institutions, institutional investors as well as other financial players. The G20 can play a constructive and supportive role in this regard. It can be a catalyst for new policy consensus, fostering high-level coordination and creative partnerships. These can boost government action and transform capital market and financial flows, thus contributing to the implementation of the United Nations Framework Convention on Climate Change and its Paris agreement. The governance of this second task force will also rely on a lean steering committee and will build on substantive work already carried out by a number of working groups of the financial track.

Reforming Global Governance

The third priority of Brazil's G20 presidency is to reinvigorate multilateralism and promote the reform of global governance institutions. In this context, we recall the Declaration on the Commemoration of the 75th anniversary of the United Nations (UNGA 75/1) which reaffirmed that our challenges are interconnected and can only be addressed through reinvigorated multilateralism, reforms and international cooperation. UN governance has not kept pace with the emergence of the Global South, and with a number of tectonic geopolitical changes, including the end of colonialism. The World Bank and the IMF governance structures do not reflect the significant contributions of developing countries and the role they play in today's global economy. The under-representation of the Global South undermines the institution's credibility and influence.

The current context of polarisation and distrust exacerbated by the conflicts in Ukraine and Palestine further weakened the very institutions that were designed to uphold international peace and security and to promote global prosperity. As Brazil's President frequently argues, it makes no sense to call on developing countries to contribute to resolving the crises the world faces without addressing their legitimate concerns. The Brazilian G20 presidency adopts the premise that only if we are in a reconfigured multilateral system can peace, stability and sustainable development be attained.

In this spirit, Brazil submitted to its counterparts in the first foreign ministers meeting in Rio de Janeiro, a proposal for a meaningful discussion on global governance reform. In support, the G20 has decided to convene a second foreign ministers' meeting at the United Nations for the first time in its history. The G20 will have a ministerial meeting at the United Nations headquarters with participation open to all UN member-states. It is scheduled to be held on the sidelines of the high-level week of the next General Assembly. It is an unprecedented opportunity for the G20 to join forces with all the UN member-states in favour of a call to action for the reform of global governance institutions, with the United Nations at its core.

Brazil's G20 presidency remains a work in progress. From its first days in December 2023, the first Sherpa meeting and the first finance track meeting have already been held, as well as a joint meeting of both tracks. We had one meeting of the working groups and the two of foreign ministers in Rio de Janeiro and of finance ministers in São Paulo. On all those occasions, Brazil has received wide support for the priorities it had established for 2024. We look forward to receiving continuous support as we move into the implementation of these priorities.

9

Vasudhaiva Kutumbakam:
A Framework for Global Cooperation

Arvind Gupta

India has set 'Vasudhaiva Kutumbakam' as the theme for its G20 presidency. The Sanskrit phrase occurs in a verse from the Maha Upanishad:

अयं निजः परो वेति गणना लघुचेतसाम्।

उदारचरितानां तु वसुधैव कुटुम्बकम्॥ (महोपनिषद्. अध्याय ४. श्लोक ७१)

(*Maha Upanishad*, chapter 4, verse 71)

Its translation reads:

"Only people with a petty outlook differentiate, saying, this is my friend and this is not my friend. But for those with a magnanimous mind, the entire world is one family."

The idea of oneness, or '*Vasudhaiva Kutumbakam*,' is also reflected in the Vedic saying '*yatra vishwambhavatiekneedam*,' that is, the "world is a nest." A similar verse is found in the *Hitopadesha*. The civilisational idea of '*Vasudhaiva Kutumbakam*' is ingrained deeply in the Indian psyche.

The theme of India's G20 presidency, '*Vasudhaiva Kutumbakam*," has a tagline which resonates with most people: 'One Earth, One Family, One Future.' This theme is highly relevant today. If the planet is to be saved from the ravages of war, climate change, alienation, and social disintegration, the people of the world must appreciate that we are in the same boat. We share the same future. There can be no winners or losers if the entire planet is destroyed due to any of the reasons I have mentioned, from ecological destruction to nuclear warfare.

Regrettably, international relations are run on the principles of narrow national interests. Universal values and ethics have little traction in the cut-throat world of strategic rivalries and destructive competition. The results are there for everyone to see – the heightened risk of the destruction of humanity and the planet. Climate change, for instance, is an existential threat, and so far, efforts to curb emissions have failed. Relentless exploitation of limited planetary resources for selfish interests has led to environmental destruction and biodiversity loss, deepening the climate crisis. In view of such realities, '*Vasudhaiva Kutumbakam*' underscores the value of the common good.

'*Vasudhaiva Kutumbakam*' does not deny the existence of national interests. It only signifies that national interests across the globe need to be aligned. There are higher goals to be pursued. It points out that a selfish pursuit of goals at the expense of others will not take one very far.

Unity in Diversity

The world is diverse, and this diversity needs to be respected. Uniformity is not natural. Approaches to solving global problems have to be inclusive. '*Vasudhaiva Kutumbakam*' underlies the respect for diversity and inclusiveness.

The timeless wisdom of Indic philosophy is that there is one truth but many paths to it. '*Ekamsat, viprabahudhavadanti*' (*Rig Veda* 1.164.46), that is, "The wise say the same truth in different ways." In fact, there is an underlying thread of unity running across this diverse world. The philosophy of Yoga, for example, underscores the unity of mind, body, and spirit. The International Day of Yoga, celebrated by every UN member-country on 21 June, reinforces the idea. Diversity cannot be suppressed.

However, there has to be harmony in diversity. Diversity should not degenerate into chaos. This kind of thinking is radically different from the exclusionary thinking that we have got used to: my way or the highway.

Respect for the other's viewpoint is critical if we have to save ourselves and the planet.

The world is experiencing the painful consequences of the Russia-Ukraine war. How can this conflict be resolved? Prime Minister Modi has often said that this should not be an era of wars. We should not be so short-sighted as to destroy ourselves knowingly. Differences should be resolved by dialogue and diplomacy. This is exactly the kind of thinking that is rooted in the philosophy of '*Vasudhaiva Kutumbakam.*' Let us realise that we are a family. War is not the solution to our problems.

In the context of climate change and environmental degradation, Prime Minister Modi has proposed Mission 'LiFe,' which stands for Lifestyle for Environment. This will require a mindset change – from extravagant living to sustainable living. However, no number of agreements and protocols will save Earth if human beings continue to follow the model of reckless consumption. The environment is being destroyed. We need an ethical and spiritual approach to save the planet. There has to be some self-restraint on consumption, some regard for those who do not have enough to eat and live and yet are victims of the excesses of those who over-consume. The rich and the elite must change their lifestyles. This requires wisdom. The philosophy of '*Vasudhaiva Kutumbakam*' is the philosophy of sustainable development.

New technologies are emerging at breakneck speed. Artificial Intelligence and quantum technology are the latest to arrive. They have fantastic use cases which can change our lives for the better. But, in this world of mutual suspicion and deep distrust, such technologies can also be manipulated for dark purposes. An unethical approach to these new technologies, driven only by strategic, economic, and financial motives, can lead to the destruction of humanity itself. In the last century, several conventions and agreements were signed to restrict the use of nuclear, chemical, and biological technologies. Today, there is talk of regulating AI and quantum technology. '*Vasudhaiva Kutumbakam*' provides the framework for new thinking on dealing with these technologies. '*Vasudhaiva Kutumbakam*' shows us that power and force must be used responsibly, in accordance with dharma and ethics.

The Case for the Global South

In the spirit of the overarching theme of G20, Prime Minister Modi has strongly advocated the cause of the Global South. The Global South is not a political or economic grouping on the international chessboard. It represents a section of humanity which is struggling to have its legitimate share of the planetary resources. A few powerful countries with access to capital and technology have cornered most resources of the Earth. Leaving behind a vast section of humanity is a recipe for disaster. '*Vasudhaiva Kutumbakam*' provides the framework for thinking about all humanity as one. It is another name for common but differentiated responsibility and climate justice – the principles that inform the UN Framework Convention on Climate Change (UNFCCC) but are sadly ignored. There are a lot of things that COVID-19 has taught us, provided we are willing to learn from it. The virtues of humility, caring, and sharing are among them. The pandemic ravaged the entire planet. Millions of lives were lost across the world. The vaccines, when invented, were cornered by a few, leading to a glaring vaccine asymmetry.

The rich countries refused to share intellectual property rights even when millions were dying. The pandemic underlined the need for healthcare for all. G20 summits have devoted a lot of attention to providing healthcare for all. That is a reflection of the value of '*Vasudhaiva Kutumbakam.*'

When faced with Nature's fury, no one is safe. This point is brought home regularly when earthquakes, forest fires, cyclones, and floods strike some or the other part of the world almost on a daily basis. Tackling disasters requires cooperation and empathy. Global problems require global cooperation. '*Vasudhaiva Kutumbakam*' is another name for global cooperation.

One should not be naïve to think that '*Vasudhaiva Kutumbakam*' is the panacea for all global problems. Wars and conflicts are all too common in global history. Billions of people have died in man-made conflicts and situations. There are still many who scoff at the values that require one to take a non-selfish approach to the world's problems. Nothing can be done about such people.

However, one can take solace in the thought that most people will not be able to deny the self-evident truth that 'Vasudhaiva Kutumbakam' is not an esoteric philosophy. It is a very practical and pragmatic way of living. To make it work requires a change of mindset from egocentric thinking to an inclusive form of thinking, informed by the spirit of selfless service. '*Vasudhaiva Kutumbakam*' signifies such an approach.

Raising the Bar for Women-led Development in G20

LAKSHMI PURI

The concept of women-led development, pioneered by Prime Minister Narendra Modi, found its eloquent expression for the first time in India's G20 presidency. The New Delhi Leaders' Declaration can go down in history as the most comprehensive and elaborate commitment to women's socio-economic empowerment – two-and-a-half pages. It included driving gender-responsive climate action; securing women's food security, nutrition and well-being; and ending violence and bias. It set a new target of reducing the gender digital gap by half by 2030 and reaching the target of reducing the labour force participation gap by 25 percent by 2025. The creation of a separate Working Group on women's empowerment is an enduring legacy enabling systematic focus and gender mainstreaming, monitoring and accountability from now on.

The G20 Delhi Summit has set new milestones and will leave valuable legacies in several respects – from being a truly people's G20 to pulling off significant deliverables for the Global South and reform of the Multilateral institutions for the 21st century. But where PM Modi has truly blazed a trail, is the way Bharat's presidency prioritized the theme of women-led development from the start, and forged unity around his Nari Shakti mission for the country and the world. It gender mainstreamed the processes and the outcomes, not just stirred in a little dose in tokenism. It also ensured impactful, intentional and perhaps the most robust and comprehensive ever G20 commitments for taking G20 and the world to a gender equal future through the G20 New Delhi Leader's Declaration.

Touchdown Points

Inspired by the pioneering Chandrayan – 3-mission touchdown point of Shiv Shakti, we could refer to six touchdown points of Delhi G20 on Nari Shakti. Most importantly, there was consecration of the concept of women-led development – PM Modi's article of faith – as an abiding G20 commitment to "enhancing women's full, effective, equal and meaningful participation as decision makers in all spheres of society, across all sectors and at all levels of the economy." There was a never seen before Jan Bhagidari – women's voice, participation and leadership in G20 decision-making, fora and events, in particular that of the grassroots women. Apart from the G20 Secretariat itself, 300000 women community leaders, artisans, SHGs, SMEs, corporates, women CSOs and activists engaged vigorously.

As rarely happens, the recommendations of Women 20 and the Gandhinagar Ministerial Conference on Women's Empowerment, were incorporated in the Delhi Summit Declaration. It is the most elaborate women's empowerment related section two-and-a-half pages in any G20 Leader's Declaration.

The women-led Development mandate includes socio-economic empowerment, equal, safe, throughout the lifecycle, access to quality, STEM, and higher education; securing women's food security, nutrition and wellbeing; driving gender inclusive climate action; enabling women's financial inclusion into the formal financial system; entrepreneurship development; full participation of women in the transitioning world of work; closing the gender pay gap; ending iniquities in care work and provisioning of affordable care infrastructure; eliminating gender-based violence in all forms and spaces and demolishing gender stereotypes, biases and discriminatory norms.

New Targets

The 18th G20 Summit raised the ambition and set new targets – halving the digital divide by 2030 and, towards that end, to adopt enabling measures and policies, funding and accelerating proven solutions. The G20 women's labour force participation gap reduction target and roadmap of 25% by 2025 and beyond is to be systematically implemented and monitored.

Taking forward the private sector Empower Initiative, concrete projects include the launch of a) Tech-equity – a platform to bring together training and information for women's upskilling into jobs and more viable businesses, b) a Mentoring Programme for women to attain more leadership positions c) launch of a call for funds to establish a regional Care Accelerator Programme to help grow innovative women's business solutions on care work.

As someone associated with the launch of the Women 20 in Ankara, I applaud the major leap in mainstreaming gender equality and women's empowerment in the institutional architecture of G20 with the creation of a Working Group on Empowerment of Women. It would have its own work stream while feeding into other sectoral working groups and Ministerial meetings, monitor the implementation of related G20 commitments and establish accountability.

Financing for Gender Equality

The most powerful economies and consequential countries of the world represented in this grouping for economic and financial management and cooperation have mustered the political will. However, the G20 members need to put the money where the pledges in Delhi Declaration are on women-led development. As committed to in Agenda 2030 for Sustainable Development and the Addis Ababa Financing for Development Declaration, substantially increased, targeted and transformative financing for gender equality and women's empowerment must be mobilized from all sources – national and international, public and private. The commitments must be aligned with the provisions in the Delhi Declaration on SDG Stimulus and acceleration plan, climate finance, MDB funding and bilateral ODA and private sector financing.

It is a time when women, particularly in developing countries, are weighed down by the cascading effects of multiple global crisis – conflicts, climate and environmental stress, poverty, food, energy and financial crisis.

There is a slide back on achieving SDG 5 and other goals and targets on gender equality and women's empowerment.

UNWOMEN, which has been supporting the G20 presidency over the years, warns that at this slow and interrupted pace of progress, these goals could take another century and more to achieve. We cannot afford humanity being shackled and unable to achieve SDGs. PM Modi and Bharat's presidency has given a clear message that as part of human centric development, women-led development must be prioritized in every way and we must touchdown on a Planet 50/50 soonest.

Agenda 2030: SDG5

As someone associated with the very idea and inclusion of Sustainable Development Goal 5 on "achieving gender equality and the empowerment of all women and girls" and with the launch of the Women20 Engagement Group in 2015 in Turkey, I am proud that PM Modi identified "women-led development" as a priority theme for India's G20 presidency. The universe seems to be coming together for India to make a pioneering contribution and lasting global contribution to one of humanity's biggest and most transformational projects of the 21st century.

In 2015, I was privileged to lead UNWOMEN to ensure that Agenda 2030 for Sustainable Development recognised that gender equality must be both a critical enabler and accelerator as well as a prime beneficiary of SDG progress. A dedicated SDG 5 on achieving gender equality and the empowerment of all women and girls with 9 targets covering following areas was adopted.

1) Ending all forms of discrimination and violence against women and harmful practices like child marriage.
2) Ensuring women's full and effective participation and equal opportunities for leadership at all levels of decision-making in political, economic, and public life.
3) Universal access to sexual and reproductive health and rights.
4) Women's equal rights to economic resources, access to ownership and control over land and other forms of property, financial services, inheritance, and natural resources.

5) Enhancing the use of enabling technology, in particular ICT to promote women's empowerment.
6) Recognising and valuing unpaid care and domestic work, through the provision of public services, infrastructure, social protection policies and burden sharing.
7) Adopt policies and enforceable laws to advance gender equality and empowerment of all women and girls at all levels.

In addition, we ensured that gender – responsive targets be included in 11 key SDGs from poverty eradication, health, education, food & nutrition, WASH, Energy, employment, economic growth, inequality to sustainable cities. The entire body of gender equality commitments in Agenda 2030 was the coping stone to what I have called a comprehensive, high standards, UN's Global Gender Equality Compact – GGEC. It builds on the motherboard of the Convention on the Elimination of the Discrimination against Women, signed by 187 countries , Beijing Platform for Action, other UN resolutions, Addis Ababa Action Agenda on Financing for Development et al.

Fortuitously, PM Modi's vision for a new India is that of achieving SDGs including SDG5. In his $ 10 trillion economy by 2030 ambition for India, women are seen as equal and indispensable actors. With a life cycle continuum approach, the Government of India has tried to ensure that women's voice and agency is supreme in India's development aspiration of an 'Atma Nirbhar Bharat' or "self-reliant India" not just for her own sake, but in the interest of the entire global community in a post-COVID world. This presents an unprecedented opportunity to decisively advance the "normative of implementation" of the UN's Global Gender Equality Compact, individually, and collectively by G20 countries and drive global action and achievement.

At the midpoint of SDGs, all UN reports point to the world being off track to achieving gender equality-related goals and targets. Daunting historical, structural economic, social, political and mindset-related barriers block progress. The COVID pandemic and now the Russia-Ukraine war has further worsened the women's economic empowerment challenges.

Women20

The W20 or the Women Engagement group has been the locus of defining and advancing the women's empowerment agenda of G20 and have done creditable work. The G20 process and Summit communique, its 10 finance and economy working groups, some dozen other work streams and 11 others Engagement Groups, the other priority themes like technological transformation, green development & LiFE and accelerated, inclusive and resilient growth, must now be gender mainstreamed and women must be equally represented in all panels/mechanisms – a task that the newly established working group on Women's empowerment will no doubt ensure. It is imperative that the G20's overarching priority of economic and financial management for global good, including crisis response which was the raison d'etre of G20, must also be gender-responsive. Most importantly, the actionable outcomes and deliverables must target accelerated achievement of gender equality.

The Way Forward

Going forward, I recommend 10-point Action plan for the G20's implementation of SDGs and the related Global Gender Equality Compact by the G20 individually, collectively and for driving global action and transformation.

i. Inspiration of the UN's GE0WE global Compact in delivering the global public goods of peace and security, human rights, humanitarian action and sustainable development – economic, social, and environmental

ii. Indivisibility: Vertical and horizontal of SDG5 and other SDGs in treatment.

iii. Integration: Involving the systematic gender mainstreaming into all key decisions, laws, policies, activities, initiatives for SDG achievement.

iv. Institutions: Creating, empowering, strengthening, and resourcing dedicated GEWE institutions at all levels – global, G20, regional, national, local, and ensuring transversal institutions are gender – responsive.

    v. Investment: Significantly increased and enhanced financial investment from all sources targeted and mainstreamed, and transformative actions for financing gender equality policies and programs.

    vi. Information: Gender-segregated Data Revolution should form the basis of the pyramid of statistics, analysis, and monitoring and 50 GEWE indicators in UN's Global Indicators framework of SDGs should be backed up.

    vii. Innovation: In all areas – socioeconomic and political and putting Science and technology/Digital/Tech 4.0 in the service of GEWE and STEM educated and skilled women and girls.

    viii. Implementation: Carrying forward and implementing reformed women's empowerment laws, policies and programs including Temporary Special Measures/ quotas etc to overcome structural barriers.

    ix. Inclusion: Bringing together multi-stakeholder actors-civil society organisations especially women's movements, faith groups, men and boys and private sector for "reengineering mindsets" and bring about behavioural change through a people's movement.

    x. Impact: G20 commitments must make actual impact – systemic and substantive in the empowerment of all women and girls – especially those most marginalised to have voice, participation and leadership in driving SDGs achievement and becoming their prime beneficiaries.

Plan of Action

Looking ahead, the successive presidencies of the G20 should take the plan of action on "bridging the gender digital divide" outlined in the New Delhi Declaration. The relevant paragraphs of the Delhi Declaration deserve to be quoted in full:

"We commit to halve the digital gender gap by 2030. To this end, we will:

    i. Address gender norms and barriers to accessibility, affordability, adoption, and usage of digital technologies.

ii.   Promote regulatory policy frameworks that enable all women and girls to actively participate in the formulation and implementation of national digital strategies, including enhancing digital literacy and skills.

iii. Identify and eliminate all potential risks that women and girls encounter from increased digitalization, including all forms of online and offline abuse, by encouraging the adoption of safety-by-design approaches in digital tools and technologies.

iv.   Promote and implement gender-responsive policies to create an enabling, inclusive, and non-discriminatory digital economy for women-led and -owned businesses, including MSMEs.

v.   Encourage and support initiatives by identifying, funding, and accelerating proven solutions, thereby improving women's livelihoods and income security.

vi.   Welcome initiatives to support women empowerment in the digital economy."

Looking ahead, the much-needed gender equality-related transformations will not happen unless the most powerful countries and economies of the world represented in the G20 show the way. India's G20 presidency should be hailed as setting new benchmarks for bringing the Ganga of women's empowerment for nourishing and rejuvenating our One Earth, One Family, One Future. By any yardstick, Bharat's G20 Presidency will go down as an outstanding achievement in the history of this preeminent global forum for economic and financial governance, and North-South development dialogue, cooperation, and decision-making. In its nearly one-year journey as well as in the destination reached, India set extraordinary benchmarks in imprinting its civilizational value of Nari Shakti which India, the G20 countries, the Global South and the rest of the world must uphold.

Global Geopolitics: India's Role as a Consensus Builder

D.B. VENKATESH VARMA

With the theme of 'Vasudhaiva Kutumbakam', or 'One Earth, One Family, One Future', which affirms the inter-connectedness of Planet Earth in the wider universe, India elevated the 2023 New Delhi Summit to the heights of success. As directed by Prime Minister Modi, the preparatory process for the Summit had included the extraordinary step of organizing meetings in all states of the country with a specific people-connect focus so much so that India's presidency was not just an event in international diplomacy but a household name in far-flung corners of the country. This new revolution in diplomacy, with an active international dimension and vibrant internal dimension, has not been seen before. However, success was not assured when India took over the presidency from Indonesia in 2022. The challenges were numerous, arising from global instability due to geopolitical conflict amongst the big powers and its negative impact on the global development agenda.

Ukraine Dilemma

The G20 Summit took place against the background of unprecedented global changes. The G20 as a grouping was conceived at a time of the financial crisis in 2008 as a dialogue forum for promoting understanding and taking common or coordinated action on specific financial and trade issues. It was not intended to be a forum for addressing bilateral or international security issues. Besides, some of the key members of the G20 had pre-existing forums for addressing these issues such as the G7. The G20 has had a good track record of productive outcomes on the issues of its original mandate – in addressing the global fallout of the 2008 financial crisis. India was keen to preserve the original mandate of the G20.

The outbreak of the Ukraine conflict in February 2022 deepened the divisions in the international community, between Russia on the one hand and the G7 on the other. The commencement of military hostilities and the imposition of unilateral sanctions by the USA and its allies had the further effect of paralyzing the United Nations Security Council and other UN bodies which have the primary responsibility for the maintenance of international peace and security. The Ukraine conflict also had a negative impact on the developmental agenda of the Global South due to disruption of fuel, fertilizer, and food supplies which further exacerbated the precarious economic, social, and debt servicing conditions of many developing countries. However, at the insistence of the G7, an unfortunate precedent was created in the Bali Declaration of the G20 Summit in 2022 of including paragraphs of a political nature in the Summit document. This enabled consensus in the Bali Summit but it was an outcome that only sharpened divisions amongst the G20 countries as to the real purpose and meaning of the grouping.

Bali Summit and Legacy

It was against this background that India took over the presidency in 2023 and was immediately faced with the headwinds of the international situation and the legacy of the Bali Summit. India has a well-articulated position on the Ukraine conflict, notably through Prime Minister Modi's call that "this is not an era of war" as communicated during his meeting with President Putin in Samarkand in 2022. However, as the host country, India had an added responsibility to build consensus considering the various and sometimes sharply differing views of members, fulfilling one of the key tasks of its presidency, which was to promote dialogue and find consensus. While the G7 wanted reiteration of the condemnation of Russia as in the Bali Declaration, Russia argued that the conflict situation had changed considerably since the last summit – including the attack on the Nord Stream pipeline and hence that formulation was not acceptable.

Against the background of such deep geopolitical splits, India's G20 team headed by its Sherpa, Amitabh Kant, and G20 Chief Coordinator Harsh Vardhan Shingla, as well as those representing India at the ministerial level, exerted vigorous efforts to promote dialogue and consensus. Even though consensus on Ukraine was elusive until the Summit, consensus was reached on a vast majority of substantive issues in key priority areas – Sustainable Development Goals (SDGs), Green Development, Multilateral Development Banks, Digital Public Infrastructure, and Gender Equality. The common ground attained in the G20 reinforced at the global level, international efforts to address challenges that concern all humanity with focus on development and growth, climate change; resilient growth; progress on SDGs; green development, and Lifestyle for Environment (LiFE); technological transformation and public digital infrastructure; reforming multilateral institutions; women-led development; and international peace and harmony. In doing so, the developmental imperative of the G20 has been further reinforced during the Indian presidency of the G20. This gave a new momentum to multilateralism, a strong voice for issues of concern to the Global South, ensured that the G7 joined as stakeholders and the overall result enhanced India's diplomatic stature and influence.

The Global South Virtual Summit

The substantive content of the G20 outcome document has been enriched by the unprecedented move by Prime Minister Modi to host in January 2023 a virtual summit of developing countries to impart a distinct Global South imprint on the G20 proceedings. This has not only changed the centre of gravity within the G20, which tended to favour the G7 towards non-G7 members but also moved the G20 in line with the general trend of multipolarity now evident in the international system. A momentous development in promoting inclusivity was India's proposal to include the African Union (AU) in the G20. With its 55 members, the AU's formal inclusion at the Delhi Summit would ensure not only in consolidating India's traditionally friendly relations with countries of the African Continent but also amplify voices of the Global South at global forums.

At a time of great power conflict and numerous global challenges, the success of India in preserving the G20 as a platform for dialogue on key issues, with the participation of key countries of the G7, Russia and China are noteworthy. India's Sherpa's call that the G20 is a development forum and not a forum for political conflict has resonated well among the G20 members.

The value of the G20 as a forum for bringing together developed and emerging economies is now widely recognized. The latter have interests and priorities that are distinct from the G7 or Russia and China and cannot allow the G20 to be taken hostage by conflicts they are not involved with. They don't wish to continue to suffer the negative consequences of a European conflict with global ramifications. The G20 push towards peace, dialogue, and diplomacy was timely. That has been India's national position from the commencement of the Ukraine conflict and has been maintained during the Sherpa dialogue process.

It is reported that the paragraphs on Ukraine were not agreed upon until the Delhi Summit while on a majority of other issues India had ensured that agreement had been reached. This was ensured by holding over 200 meetings in 60 cities during which all the delegations had ample opportunities to find common ground. Therefore, the overall value of the G20 summit document was enhanced, giving all members a prior stake in a successful outcome. Despite contrary pressures, India held an open but firm negotiating stance as host on the contentious paragraphs relating to Ukraine. It is said that more than 250 iterations of the draft paragraphs were discussed during the last week preceding the Summit thus testing not only the patience and diplomatic skills of all delegations but of the host, India, which is responsible for negotiation of the document. As India was committed at the highest level to an inclusive, ambitious, decisive, and action-oriented Leaders Declaration to be issued at the September Summit, no stone was left unturned.

Negotiating the Consensus

In the event, consensus was reached through a compromise that was made possible only because India and Russia agreed to a more detailed language in the New Delhi Declaration as compared to the Bali Declaration, which was a key demand of the G7, as long as the condemnation of Russia was removed. The USA for its part helped in toning down expectations of its G7 partners, many of whom had hardline positions, to secure more forward-leaning language on the Ukraine conflict, including references in paragraphs 9 to 14; call on all states to refrain from the threat or use of force to seek territorial acquisition against the territorial integrity, sovereignty or political independence of any state; that the use of threat of use of nuclear weapons is inadmissible; refence to the Black Sea Initiative; cessation of military destruction of relevant infrastructure and the welcoming of all relevant and constructive initiatives that support a comprehensive, just and durable peace in Ukraine that will uphold all the purposes and principles of the UN Charter for the promotion of peaceful, friendly and good neighbourly relations among all the nations in the spirit of 'One Earth, One family, One Future.' There was also reference to PM Modi's statement that the present is not an era of war.

The consensus was made possible due to several factors. Under PM Modi's leadership, it was made known that the G20 summit was of the highest priority for India and the Global South. Therefore, the stakes were not just limited to the G20 issues, but it was made clear that a failure would have an impact on bilateral relations as well. Secondly, not only was an intense preparatory process put in place, which gave ample opportunity for delegations to air their views, but every effort was made to expand the areas of common agreement so that the size of the overall 'cake' was larger, thus creating an added incentive for members to support a consensus document. Thirdly, India stood its ground on the contentious issue of Ukraine without being swayed to one side or the other. This created trust in the host's efforts to find a compromise. The compromise itself was well drafted with an optimal balance between specificity and ambiguity – a formula that might not have made all countries happy but made sure that the level of unhappiness of anyone was not strong enough to break consensus. India also created coalitions such as those of the troika of the G20 chairs, which ensured that India was never alone in pushing for a consensus. Lastly, in terms of negotiating tactics, India chose the right timing drawing the line on negotiations, with PM Modi announcing on the first day itself that consensus had been reached. This announcement was greeted with applause.

Conclusion

It is widely recognized that India as the Chair left no stone unturned to find a consensus and had performed an outstanding job. India's global standing has been assured by its hosting of the G20 Summit. This would be remembered as a major milestone in India's diplomatic history and a turning point in our international engagement. At a time when geopolitics threatened to disrupt the international agenda, India's leadership of the G20 at a crucial time resulted in not only the development agenda being preserved but also strengthened in the face of grave geopolitical disturbances. Crucially, the character of the G20 has changed from a grouping dominated by G7 concerns to one that is now better prepared to address a more equitable international cooperative agenda that is sensitive to the interests of the Global South. At a time when many multilateral institutions have fallen victim to geopolitical conflicts, preserving the original agenda of the G20 as an effective, inclusive, and action-oriented international forum is a lasting contribution and legacy of India's Presidency of the G20 under PM Modi's leadership.

SECTION 2

GLOBAL SOUTH AND AFRICA

12

Africa G20 Moment

Anil Sooklal

India assumed the G20 Presidency at a very challenging period in modern human history. Not since the end of the Cold War has the world been so fractured and polarised as a result of several simultaneous challenges. Thomas Friedman has described the current era as the 'Age of Acceleration.' Several global issues are cascading on the human psyche, all at the same time, creating a dilemma on how to effectively address these challenges simultaneously. These include the advent of new technologies, climate change, biodiversity loss, as well as globalisation. More recently, the impact of the COVID pandemic as well as the Russia-Ukraine conflict have collectively contributed to a devastating impact on the global community.

All the above issues received attention within the G20 agenda. However, the impact of these challenges is felt most among the most vulnerable countries, especially the Least Developed (LDCs) and Small Island Developing States (SIDS) as well as Africa. In Africa itself, over 30 million people were pushed into extreme poverty in 2021 and about 22 million jobs were lost due to the pandemic. Furthermore, the Russia-Ukraine conflict is expected to push another 1.8 million Africans into extreme poverty in 2022 rising to over 2.3 million in 2023. The dire plight of developing countries in containing and addressing the severe impact of the pandemic and the conflict as well as the challenges posed by climate change must receive priority attention in the G20 Development Agenda under India's presidency. India as a developing country must prioritise the development agenda and ensure that it assumes centre-stage within the

G20. The Global South will look to India to ensure that issues of development that are critical in advancing their development, including meeting the UN Sustainable Development Goals (SDGs), receive priority attention in the G20 in 2023.

Development Agenda

In 2010, the G20 leaders identified the need to establish the G20 DWG with a mandate to lead in the implementation of the group's development agenda. At the Seoul Summit in November 2010, G20 leaders adopted the multi-year action plan on Development and the Seoul Development Consensus for Shared Growth. These two documents guide the work of the DWG. South Africa serves as a permanent co-chair of the DWG since its inception. Since 2010, each successive presidency of the G20 has placed specific development issues as the core focus of the DWG during its presidency, whilst also following up on commitments already made. The Comprehensive Accountability Report released in 2013 for the first time served to inform on G20 commitments annually, namely, an update of the G20 Action Plan and an assessment of the progress on the development commitments undertaken by G20 leaders.

AU's Agenda 2063

How has Africa benefited from the G20's programs and commitments in addressing its developmental challenges? South Africa is the only African country that is a G20 member. The Chair of the African Union (AU) and the Chair of the African Union Development Agency – New Partnership for Africa's Development (AUDA–NEPAD) both serve on the G20 as observers. Within the G20, South Africa has consistently advocated the advancement of the AU's Agenda 2063.

Since its inception, the DWG has become an important instrument in addressing the most critical development challenges of the Global South, including Africa. DWG programs over the years have focused on a whole range of development issues including human resource development, women's economic empowerment, climate action, infrastructure, green energy, food security, industrialisation, digitalisation, trade, private investments, as well as job creation. The 2012 progress report of the DWG notes that the G20 must serve as a relevant coordination forum for international economic cooperation. Effective contributions by international organisations and G20 countries, supported by concerted actions of G20 members are fundamental to supporting national efforts of developing countries in overcoming hunger and poverty and promoting sustainable development.

Following repeated calls by South Africa as well as the Chairs of the AU and the AUDA-NEPAD for Africa's development agenda to receive support from the G20, there emerged an Africa-specific program in the DWG under the Chinese and German presidencies of the G20, respectively, in 2016 and 2017.

The G20 Leaders Summit in Hangzhou, China, in September 2016 launched the G20 initiative on supporting industrialisation in Africa and Least Developed Countries. This initiative was welcomed by African countries as it addressed a critical gap in Africa's economic regeneration. Although this was a voluntary initiative that has had a limited direct impact in addressing Africa's industrialisation, it nonetheless brought sharp focus on the need of the global community to partner in Africa's industrialisation.

The Hangzhou Leaders Summit notes, *"We launched the G20 initiative on supporting industrialization in Africa and LDCs to strengthen their inclusive growth and development potential through voluntary actions."* To date, not much has been achieved in advancing Africa's industrialisation through the G20 Hangzhou commitment as it relies on voluntary actions.

An equally important initiative meant to advance Africa's development was launched during the German presidency of the G20, namely, the Compact with Africa (CwA). It was initiated to promote private investments in Africa including in infrastructure.

The CwA's primary objective is to increase the attractiveness of private investments through substantial improvements of the macro business and financing frameworks. It seeks to bring together reform-minded African countries, international organisations, and bilateral partners from the G20 and beyond to coordinate country-specific reform agendas, support respective policy measures, and advertise investment opportunities to the private sector. The initiative is demand-driven and open to all African countries.

To date, only 12 African countries are party to the CwA. The question arises as to why so few African countries have become part of the CwA given the benefits it professes to accrue to CwA members. According to the CwA 2022 monitoring report, the outlook for CwA countries is relatively better than global and regional projections. As a group, CwA countries are expected to continue to grow despite headwinds arising from the conflict in Ukraine, potential scarring from the ongoing pandemic, and the intensification of the food and fuel shocks that are already underway.

It is obvious that most African countries are reluctant to join the CwA which despite being launched some five years ago has had a very limited impact in addressing the continent's investment needs. Part of the challenge pertains to the so-called country-specific reform agenda of the CwA which is seen by African countries as an intrusive mechanism.

South-South Solidarity

India and Africa have a shared history spanning several centuries of robust economic, trade, cultural, and people-to-people exchanges. In more recent times, India was one of the chief architects of the first Asia-Africa Conference held in Bandung, Indonesia, in April 1955. It was at Bandung that the foundations of South-South solidarity and cooperation were firmly laid. Since its independence in 1947, development diplomacy has become an integral part of India's foreign policy. Over the years India has strengthened its historical ties with Africa through a network of bilateral, trilateral, and multilateral engagements. The India Africa Forum Summit (IAFS) is now an established and important platform for advancing India-Africa relations.

Through its bilateral engagements with Africa, including the AU Commission in Addis Ababa as well as the IAFS, India has a vibrant and multifaceted development cooperation engagement with Africa. Prime Minister Modi's Ten-Point Plan is aligned with the AU's Agenda 2063. It is through this prism that one must view India's G20 presidency and its engagement with Africa. As a trusted time-honoured partner of Africa and a fellow developing country of the Global South, there is an expectation that Africa's development agenda will be one of the priority focus areas of India's presidency. This sentiment was articulated by India's G20 Sherpa,

Amitabh Kant, while addressing the Kigali Global Dialogue held in Rwanda in August 2022. He noted that India will embed the concerns of the developing world at the heart of the G20 Agenda. He further stated that the development concerns of Africa must form the bedrock of the G20 consensus. He also highlighted that India and African nations collectively have the highest percentage of young populations in the world. This demographic dividend needs to be leveraged responsibly to ensure that it achieves its highest potential.

India's commitment and solidarity with Africa were sharply demonstrated at the height of the pandemic through its Vaccine Maitri initiative. While most of the developed world was focused on ensuring vaccines for its citizens which led to many of these countries being accused of vaccine nationalism and vaccine hoarding, India made available vaccines for free or at a marginal cost to the developing world, including Africa.

India's theme for its G20 Presidency, *Vasudhaiva Kutumbakam: One Earth, One Family, One Future,* resonates with the African concept of Ubuntu: 'I am because you are; to be human is to recognise the humanity of others.' It is these twin concepts that place the well-being of humanity at its centre that should underpin the India-Africa cooperation and partnership within the G20 and beyond. The priorities identified by India for its presidency cover the key issues needing global attention and collaboration. These include issues that will also be transformational to Africa, namely, health, agriculture, education, digitalisation, climate financing, food security, disaster risk reduction, and multilateral reforms.

The Rise of Africa

India's Presidency of the G20 in 2023 reasserted the centrality of the G20 in addressing critical global issues in an inclusive and cooperative manner. In a world plagued by poly-crisis many sceptics doubted India's ability to deliver a successful and substantive G20 Summit. The G20 New Delhi Leaders Declaration is one of the most comprehensive and substantial G20 Declarations ever issued. The New Delhi Declaration demonstrated India's leadership role by fostering consensus, bridging the gap between the Global North and South and bringing to the fore the emergence of the Global South and Africa. The Global South Summit under India's leadership brought attention to the Global South as a cohesive and powerful force in shaping the evolving international architecture.

However, one of the most important outcomes of India's G20 Presidency was the inclusion of the African Union as a full member of the G20. History will record the important role played by India and more especially its astute and respected leader, Prime Minister Narendra Modi's personal role in championing the inclusion of the African Union as a full member of the G20. The role of India in this regard has been widely applauded by the African leadership as a whole. The inclusion of the African Union as a G20 member bears testimony to a continent on the rise and no global formation of significance can ignore the inclusion of Africa as a critical voice in addressing global issues. The AU will assume its rightful place alongside member-countries and the EU in the G20, transiting from an invited observer to an equal member of the G20. The AU, together with South Africa, the only African country that is a member of the G20, will together be able to advance the African Agenda of the Continent in a more cohesive and powerful manner ensuring that issues pertaining to the continent are mainstreamed and receive the rightful attention they deserve. The addition of the AU to the G20 family further strengthens this critical global body and enriches its ability to act in a more inclusive manner in addressing the multitude of challenges we face in a highly fractured and polarised world. In such an environment India has demonstrated that the G20 can be a force for global good and it is possible to bridge our differences in working together for the well-being of humanity as one global family, namely, One Earth, One Family, One Future.

Africa, India, South Africa and the Global South in G20

ELIZABETH SIDIROPOULOS

Prime Minister Narendra Modi's request to his G20 counterparts in June 2023 to invite the African Union to become a permanent member of the grouping finally fructified after years of vacillation at the G20 summit in New Delhi in September 2023. The inclusion of the AU in G20 was a bold step that vocalised the views of many in Africa and beyond about the importance of having a collective African voice at the G20 table. The G20 is not the UN; it is an exclusive, select group. The value of such a small grouping is that it can build consensus among systemically important countries on key global challenges. The downside is that it may ignore, knowingly or unknowingly, the potential consequences of its decisions on the most vulnerable economies.

Africa is home to 33 of the world's least developed countries. About a third of its population lived below the extreme poverty line in 2022 (431 million people). Achieving sustainable development is an existential necessity for these people. Many African countries are unlikely to meet all the SDGs by 2030. In many cases, there is insufficient credible or timely data for effective monitoring and policymaking. Coupled with the imperative of an energy transition, the scale of resources needed to achieve the SDGs runs into trillions of dollars.

These challenges cannot be dealt with only through domestic policymaking. They also require a global architecture geared towards effective financing for development. And this is where the G20's mandate as the world's premier global economic governance forum becomes crucial for the continent and indeed all of the Global South.

Hence, the inclusion of the AU in G20 at the New Delhi summit serves as more than a symbolic gesture. The AU's full participation in the G20 would increase the output legitimacy of the club, while also providing a platform for a continent that is under-represented in the G20.

Why AU Matters

The African Union and the NEPAD heads of state implementation committee had been granted observer status at the G20 soon after the grouping was elevated to summit level in 2008. During the global financial crisis South Africa, as the only African member of the G20, working together with the African Development Bank, created a platform for consultation with other African states to coordinate positions on the crisis response. More recently, as the COVID pandemic was breaking out across the world and countries were locking down in early 2020, the G20 under the Saudi presidency was meeting to discuss this unprecedented health crisis and take remedial action. One of the most critical issues was how to deal with the many indebted developing countries for which the pandemic was accelerating their fiscal trauma. SA, that at the time, was both AU chair and a G20 member, convened a meeting of the AU Bureau, and included a number of African institutions such as the AfDB and the African Centre for Disease Control and Prevention, to discuss and take to the G20 meeting in March 2020 the African concerns and proposals.

South Africa has often been considered by many external actors as representing the continent in such forums, an expectation that is not placed on the other G20 members. Whenever possible, it has advocated for African issues but it is there in the first instance to defend its own interests. Including more African voices is a positive step, but the path will not be smooth.

Capacity Building

For the AU's G20 membership to be effective, the AU and its member-states will have to ensure there is the requisite technical expertise and capacity, as well as a sufficiently wide mandate for the AU (through the rotating chair and the Commission Chair) to meaningfully advocate for certain outcomes and for agenda-setting. This is important because the AU is an intergovernmental organisation. The AU Commission does not have the same legal competencies as the European Commission. Nevertheless, over the last decade, the AU has been able to develop common positions on certain critical global issues such as climate change. This approach creates a foundation upon which to build to ensure the AU's meaningful engagement in the G20.

Since independence, India has considered itself a leader of the South, both through the Non-Aligned Movement and also through its bilateral South-South cooperation initiatives. South Africa, since the end of apartheid, has also positioned itself very strongly as a leader on advocating for Global South issues, South-South cooperation and African priorities. There have been numerous examples of cooperation between them on Global South issues over the years. In the late 1990s, both countries advocated for the removal of intellectual property rules that restricted access to ARVs for low and middle-income countries under WTO's TRIPS, a fight which they won. During the COVID-19 pandemic, India and South Africa made a formal submission to the WTO in October 2020 for a temporary waiver on all patents, trade secrets, industrial designs, and copyrights on corona virus related drugs, vaccines, diagnostics, and other medical technologies during the pandemic. This would enable all countries to have affordable access to critical medical supplies. The proposal has met with only partial success at the WTO, but it is nevertheless an important step in rethinking existing rules related to public health versus private gain.

In 2023, at the start of its G20 presidency, India held a virtual summit – Voices of the Global South – to which all Global South countries that were not G20 members were invited. Its objective was to 'provide a common platform to deliberate on the concerns, interests and priorities that affect the developing countries' (as set out by the Ministry of External Affairs) and to channel them into the G20 deliberations. India followed it up with a second virtual summit of the Global Summit shortly before the formal conclusion of India's G20 presidency in November 2023.

Debt Distress

Together with the IMF and the World Bank, India co-chaired the Global Sovereign Debt Roundtable in April 2023 to discuss debt sustainability and debt restructuring challenges and ways to address them, given the slow progress in the G20's Common Framework. The objective is to identify actions that can be taken quickly to accelerate debt restructuring processes, making them more efficient. This is a critical undertaking although progress continues to be slow because of the difficulty of bringing the variety of debtors on board – both public and private.

Both countries and other BRICS members have pushed for the reform of the Bretton Woods institutions so that they can better serve the needs of the developing world. Sovereign debt and climate finance have been high on South Africa's list of areas requiring significant changes in the global financial architecture. Reform of the UN Security Council and the UN as a whole to better reflect the rise of Global South countries has also been a common priority. The challenge that needs to be overcome there is that of restoring the UN's credibility and overcoming the paralysis that is a feature of the growing geopolitical contestation.

G20, a Bridge-Builder

In that vein, both South Africa and India want to ensure that a forum such as the G20 remains a place where consensus can be forged on critical global economic governance issues. This means trying to safeguard it from the geopolitical rivalries that have become more pronounced over the last two years. Major global challenges such as climate change, poverty and inequality should not be forgotten. In the area of climate change, it is clear that time is running out for the planet. Preserving the G20 as a bridge between North and South, between geopolitical rivals and rich and poor is an essential ingredient for tackling the transnational crises facing the world. From 2022 to 2025 four leading Global South countries are presiding over the G20 (Indonesia, India, Brazil and South Africa). It is a once-in-a-lifetime opportunity to ensure that development is at the heart of the agenda and that the voices of those who are most vulnerable find their way into the discussions and the outcomes.

Delhi's G20 Legacy: Empowering and Elevating Africa

RAJIV BHATIA

*Developing countries have had enough ... Enough of paying for a climate
crisis they did nothing to cause. Enough of sky-high interest rates and
debt defaults. And enough of life-and-death decisions about their people
that are taken beyond their borders, without their views and their voices.*[1]

António Guterres, United Nations Secretary-General

From championing the anti-colonial struggle and emancipation from
racial discrimination to launching the Non-Aligned Movement
(NAM), from founding the Group of 77 on developmental issues to
promoting South-South cooperation and the North-South dialogue, India
has maintained a consistent policy, while leading from the front. Given
this sterling record, it was not surprising that India's G20 presidency was
marked by a blend of creativity and enthusiasm with which the nation
advocated the cause of the Global South and secured the admission of the
African Union (AU) as a permanent member of the G20. These twin
achievements will be remembered for long as reflecting India's valuable
legacy and contribution to the development of G20. India's presidency
strengthened the forum by making it more inclusive and representative.

About the decision on AU's entry into G20, two aspects were
particularly remarkable: one, the quiet, behind-the-scenes diplomatic work
by India, with the help of a few like-minded countries that overcame
reservations and resistance from certain G20 members; and two, its swift

implementation. Within minutes of the opening of the New Delhi summit on 9 September 2023, Prime Minister Narendra Modi invited Azali Assoumani, President of the Union of Comoros and Chairperson of the AU, to take his place at the main conference table. The dignitary, escorted by India's External Affairs Minister, S. Jaishankar, walked forward and was warmly embraced by the G20 President. That spontaneous embrace vividly reflected the rise of the Global South and the recognition of Africa's centrality within it.

Backdrop

G20, the world's premier forum for international economic cooperation, evolved significantly under India's presidency that ran from 1 December 2022 to November 2023. Fifteen years the first Leaders Summit (Washington, November 2008), India hosted the 18th in September 2023. It was an unprecedented responsibility, given the complex geopolitical, economic and climate change-related challenges faced by the world. While different constituencies within the G20 and outside were busy promoting their respective agendas, New Delhi – driven by its faith in strategic autonomy – could be relied upon to adopt a balanced and inclusive strategy. Harsh Vardhan Shringla, India's G20 Chief Coordinator and former foreign secretary, accurately predicted the nation's essential approach to the presidency:

> India's wide acceptability in the international community, strong developing country credentials, independence in thought and action and resilient scientific and economic base have uniquely positioned it to provide global leadership at a critical time in international affairs.[2]

India was resolved to do justice to its diverse responsibilities as the steward of the forum, which was composed of G7 nations, the European Union (EU), and 12 other countries. There was little doubt that the interests of the developing world, especially Africa, would figure high on India's list of priorities. This essay focuses attention on Africa – the heart of the Global South – and the developing world in general, and its relative marginalisation in the work of G20 before the presidency was given to India. It presents an objective analysis of how the Indian leadership ensured the mainstreaming of the South's vital concerns while serving as a powerful bridge between the developed and developing segments of our planet.

Africa and G20

A critical perusal of the Leaders' Declaration and related documents of past summits between 2008 and 2022 shows that developing countries, especially in Africa, received minimal attention. There have, however, been at least four notable exceptions to this trend.

First, the Seoul Summit (November 2010) took a clear-cut line that the goal to narrow the development gap and reduce poverty was integral to achieving strong, sustainable, and balanced growth of the world economy. The trick, it underscored, was to create new poles of growth and contribute to global balancing. It proclaimed the 'Seoul Development Consensus for Shared Growth', with its advocacy of six core principles,[3] including a responsible partnership between G20 and the Low-Income Countries (LICs). The leaders agreed on nine key pillars, that is, the areas where actions were needed to remove bottlenecks for resilient growth in developing countries. Even a 'Multi-Year Action Plan on Development' was proposed.[4] However, little of the Seoul outcome was heard in subsequent years.

Second, the Hamburg Summit (July 2017) singled out Africa for exclusive attention due to its "recognition of the opportunities and challenges in African countries as well as the goals of the 2030 Agenda."[5] It launched the 'G20 Africa Partnership' which hinged on promises of enhanced investment from G7 countries against noticeable improvement in investment and business framework in willing African partners. 'Investment Compacts' were agreed to by seven African countries: Cote d'Ivoire, Ethiopia, Ghana, Morocco, Rwanda, Senegal, and Tunisia. Later, this number increased to 12. The annexure to the declaration detailed key elements of this partnership and the process to be followed.[6] A stand-alone G20 Africa Partnership Conference was held in Berlin in June 2017, which created a buzz. Regrettably, follow-up results proved disappointing.

Third, the Osaka Summit (June 2019) raised hopes of Africa receiving special treatment, given Japan's extensive role in creating close links with

Africa since the 1990s. However, Japan's presidency restricted itself to extending only broad support to developing countries in their efforts to achieve progress towards the timely implementation of the Sustainable Development Goals (SDGs) and reiterating its continued support to the Compact with Africa (CwA).[7]

Finally, under Indonesia's presidency (2021–22), a G20 roadmap was created for stronger recovery and resilience in developing countries including the Least Developed Countries (LDCs) and Small Island Developing States (SIDS). It spelt out three focus areas, namely, Micro, Small and Medium-sized Enterprises (MSMEs), adaptive social protection, and green economy, including blue economy through climate-resilient development.[8] The Bali Summit Declaration referred to Africa: "We also reiterate our continued support to Africa, including through the G20 Compact with Africa and the G20 Initiative on Supporting Industrialization in Africa and LDCs."[9]

What Africa Needs

What is needed from the G20 leadership is more than mere words to encourage Africa. The African continent is home to 17 per cent of the world's population. Yet it accounts for about 4 per cent of the global GDP. More specifically, Sub-Saharan Africa (SSA) comprises low, lower-middle, upper-middle, and high-income countries, 22 of which are "fragile or conflict-affected", and 13 are small states "characterized by a small population, limited human capital, and a confined land area".[10] Their economies were badly affected by the triple shocks of COVID-19, the general economic slowdown, and the war in Ukraine. The World Bank stated that SSA economies were impacted by "higher commodity prices, higher food, fuel, and headline inflation, tightening of global financial conditions, and reduced financing flows into the region."[11]

Africa's needs, aspirations, and plans are well-known to those who regularly monitor African developments and are open to listening to African voices. The continent's development perspective has been fully delineated in the AU's Agenda 2063 and the UN's 2030 Agenda for Sustainable Development. Cyril Ramaphosa, President of South Africa, wrote, "We believe there is a need for Africa to be fully involved in decision-making on global political, economic, financial, security, environmental and health governance."[12]

The COVID era drew the world's attention to two issues in particular: the vaccine injustice to Africa where the availability of COVID vaccines and medicines was far lower than in developed and emerging economies; and the indebtedness which grew in serious proportion. Through its laudable support for the Debt Service Suspension Initiative (DSSI), G20 attempted to provide much-needed relief. But its results remained well below the level of expectations generated earlier. Besides, the African Continental Free Trade Area (AfCFTA) saw its launch delayed during the COVID era when Africa's external partners were distracted and busy with their own problems or those of other regions.

Africa clamoured for effective relief from the escalating debt and interest burden. Moreover, it needed support for its development needs covering diverse sectors such as infrastructure, agriculture and food security, healthcare, education and capacity building, job creation, and safeguards against climate change. An effective way to help Africa was to increase its weight in the G20. Africa, composed of 54 countries, represents 27 per cent of the total member-states (193) of the UN. Hence, it deserved to be represented better in the G20. One seat, held by South Africa, was simply not enough. This author was among the earliest advocates in India of the proposal to admit the AU into G20.[13]

Paul Martin, former prime minister of Canada, provided an irrefutable rationale for the AU becoming a permanent voice at the G20 table. He wrote:

> As our issues get more complex, the table must be more inclusive. Solving our problems and navigating a way forward involves more cooperation and collaboration, nothing less. Expanding the table and listening to more voices is more difficult than with a small group of like-minded participants, but it is the only way to forge collective action against global challenges.[14]

During 2015-19, India made special efforts to befriend Africa. Spelling out the ten guiding principles that shaped India's Africa policy, PM Modi stated before the Ugandan parliament, "Africa will be at the top of our priorities." He conveyed to the African side that the India-Africa development partnership would be "guided by your priorities." India's friends in Africa, therefore, became hopeful that as the president of G20 for the year 2022–23, India would do its utmost to support Africa's interests in this forum.

From Africa to the Global South

However, this Africa-focused approach needed to be placed in the larger global context. True to its self-image as an aspiring leading power, India has the responsibility to take care of the interests of friendly countries in other regions too such as the Indian Ocean region, South Asia, Central Asia, Southeast Asia, South Pacific, and Latin America. Taken together with Africa, this entire space is best represented by the 'Global South.' This is a term that Nour Dados and Raewyn Connell depict below:

> The term 'Global South' functions as more than a metaphor for underdevelopment. It references an entire history of colonialism, neo-imperialism, and differential economic and social change through which large inequalities in living standards, life expectancy, and access to resources are maintained.[15]

While being fully supportive of critical elements of the African agenda, India needed to balance the diverse dimensions of its responsibilities as the president of G20. It was natural for India to position itself as one of the foremost leaders of the Global South, and its intentions leaned in that direction. Sujan Chinoy, chair of the Think-20 Core Group of India's G20 presidency, wrote presciently, "India will work to deliver global goods as a voice of the Global South," stressing that the "development agenda must receive the first billing."[16]

Four-step Strategy

In retrospect, it is evident that India as the president of G20 devised a four-step strategy for achieving optimal success in its pursuit of the diverse interests of the Global South.

First, the Voice of the Global South Summit (VOGSS) was hosted by India in virtual format on 12–13 January 2023. Its theme was 'Unity of voice, Unity of purpose.' A total of 125 countries took part in it. The host's purpose was to obtain extensive input about the priorities, perspectives and concerns of the developing world. This summit also allowed the government to showcase India's experiences through simple, scalable and sustainable solutions relating to vaccine development, digital public goods, financial inclusion, and last-mile connectivity.

Second, at the deliberations of the G20 working groups and ministerial meetings, a firm eye was kept on the views and expectations of the Global South. This explains why the New Delhi Leaders Declaration (NDLD) amply reflected the developing world's views on economic growth, climate change, accelerating the achievement of SGDs, and the wide use of digital technology for development purposes. According to some calculations, over 50 per cent content of the summit declaration aimed to benefit developing countries.

Further, through a highly substantive paragraph (No. 76), the G20 leaders expressed their belief that the "inclusion of the African Union into the G20 will significantly contribute to addressing the global challenges of our time." It added, "Africa plays an important role in the global economy. We commit to strengthen our ties with and support the African Union to realise the aspirations under Agenda 2063. We also reiterate strong support to Africa, including through the G20 Compact with Africa and G20 Initiative on supporting industrialization in Africa and LDCs."[17]

Para 79 stated, "We will continue to integrate the perspectives of the developing countries into the G20 agendas and appreciate the G20 members' initiatives in this regard."[18]

Third, as a sequel to the first VOGSS, India hosted its second edition in virtual format on 17 November 2023. The theme this time was 'Global South: Together for Everyone's Growth, Everyone's Trust.' This was an occasion for the presidency to apprise the Global South leaders of how their views moulded the New Delhi Summit decisions. Participants expressed their appreciation for India's efforts in strengthening the voice of the Global South and galvanising concrete G20 actions for the benefit of the developing world.

Finally, at the virtual G20 follow-up summit held on 17 November

2023, a special push was given for the effective implementation of various G20 decisions. Addressing it, PM Modi stated, "The 21st century will have to give top priority to the concerns of the Global South moving forward."[19]

What Next?

Evaluating the achievements of India's presidency a few months after its conclusion, one can visualise a strategy that is needed for the immediate future. The present G20 Troika comprising India, Brazil and South Africa has a responsibility to concentrate on careful implementation of the decisions taken. Brazil's presidency may have its priorities, but this needs to be pursued within the agreed framework that helps the Global South in general and Africa in particular. For this purpose, effective coordination among the IBSA countries mentioned above is essential. Instead of adding novel ideas, they should work out a practical plan of action for the international community to deliver on the commitments made.

In this context, the role of Brazil as the current G20 president is particularly important. Ambassador Jorge Arguello, the Argentinian Sherpa, writing in 2023, pointed out that the presidencies of India and Brazil would be 'at the forefront', with the G20 agenda reflecting 'the interests and aspirations of the Global South.' He added, "Their presidencies of the G20 can demonstrate that the Global South is ready to take on the global economic governance agenda in a pluralistic and inclusive manner."[20]

Finally, India's responsibilities do not end here. New Delhi needs to carry forward its agenda of deepening cooperation with Africa at three levels – bilateral, regional and pan-African. Convening of the fourth India-Africa Forum Summit is now highly desirable. At the same time, increased attention needs to be given to other regions of the Global South. In this scenario, the recently launched DAKSHIN (Development and Knowledge Sharing Initiative) of the Global South Centre of Excellence, New Delhi, may have a pioneering role to play.

NOTES

1. United Nations. 'Warning Over Half of World Is Being Left Behind, Secretary-General Urges Greater Action to End Extreme Poverty, at Sustainable Development Goals Progress Report Launch,' *UN Press*, 25 April 2023, https://press.un.org/en/2023/sgsm21776.doc.htm.

2. Harsh Vardhan Shringla. 'HTLS 2022: Drafting a blueprint to provide constructive global leadership', *Hindustan Times*, 7 November 2022.

3. 'The Seoul Summit Document', G20 Research Group, 12 November 2010, para 50, http://www.g20.utoronto.ca/2010/g20seoul-doc.html

4. 'Annex II: Multi-Year Action Plan on Development', G20 Research Group, 12 November 2010, Seoul, http://www.g20.utoronto.ca/2010/g20seoul-development.html

5. 'G20 Leaders' Declaration: Shaping an Interconnected World', G20 Research Group, 8 July 2017, Hamburg, http://www.g20.utoronto.ca/2017/2017-G20-leaders-declaration.html

6. 'Annex to G20 Leaders Declaration G20 Africa Partnership', G20 Research Group, 8 July 2017, Hamburg, http://www.g20.utoronto.ca/2017/2017-g20-annex-partnership-africa.html

7. 'G20 Osaka Leaders' Declaration', G20 Research Group, Osaka, Japan, 29 June 2019, para 27. http://www.g20.utoronto.ca/2019/2019-g20-osaka-leaders-declaration.html

8. For details, see: 'G20 Roadmap for Stronger Recovery and Resilience in Developing Countries, including Least Developed Countries and Small Island Developing States', G20 Indonesia 2022. http://www.g20.utoronto.ca/2022/G20-Roadmap-for-Stronger-Recovery-and-Resilience-in-Developing-Countries-including-Least-Developed-Countries.pdf

9. 'G20 Bali Leaders' Declaration', G20 Research Group, Bali, 16 November 2022, http://www.g20.utoronto.ca/2022/221116-declaration.html

10. 'The World Bank in Africa', The World Bank, https://www.worldbank.org/en/region/afr/overview

11. Ibid.

12. Cyril Ramaphosa. 'Reclaiming the development agenda at the G20', G20 – India, The New Delhi Summit, GT Media Group Ltd., London (2023).

13. Rajiv Bhatia. 'India, the G20 and an African agenda', Gateway House, 17 September 2020, https://www.gatewayhouse.in/india-g20-african-agenda/

14. Paul Martin. 'What is the role of the G20 in 2023?', G20 – India, The New Delhi Summit, GT Media Group Ltd., London (2023).

15. Nour Dados and Raewyn Connell. 'The Global South', https://journals.sagepub.com/doi/pdf/10.1177/1536504212436479

16. Sujan R. Chinoy. 'A voice for Global South', *The Indian Express,* 9 November 2022.

17. 'G20 New Delhi Leaders' Declaration', https://www.mea.gov.in/bilateral-documents.htm?dtl/37084/G20_New_Delhi_Leaders_Declaration

18. Ibid.

19. 'Prime Minister's Inaugural Statement at the Virtual G20 Summit', 22 November 2023, https://www.narendramodi.in/prime-minister-narendra-modis-opening-remarks-at-g20-virtual-summit-576201

20. Jorge Arguello. 'The Hour for Emerging Countries', in Iqbal Singh Sevea, Amitendu Palit and Vinod Rai (eds.), *India and the Future of G20: Shaping Policies for a Better World*, Bloomsbury India, New Delhi, 2023, pp. 21–22.

15

Rise of the Global South:
A Catalyst for a New World Order

MANISH CHAND

The ongoing resurgence of the Global South and its increasing role in setting the global governance agenda is the unfolding phenomenon of our times. In many ways, India's G20 presidency underscored the centrality of the Global South to the creation of an inclusive, responsive, responsible, and sustainable world order. This unprecedented focus on the issues and challenges of the Global South constitutes the lasting legacy of India's G20 presidency, which is expected to be carried forward not only by the successive G20 presidencies of Brazil and South Africa, but also by other G20 countries, including the developed economies of the G7. It is a paradigm shift in the forging of the global agenda, and an irreversible one at that.

India's G20 presidency, which culminated in the joint New Delhi Declaration, showcased India's role as a leading power in placing the Global South at the centre of global decision-making. The Declaration underlined that a wide array of cross-cutting challenges such as sustainable development, inclusive growth, climate change, food security, digital divide, and reform of global governance institutions cannot be undertaken without the proactive participation of the developing countries. India's G20 Sherpa Amitabh Kant encapsulated the historic importance of the New Delhi Declaration in his remarks at the briefing by India's G20 presidency on 10 September 2023. "No document of G20 has had such an immense focus on developing and emerging markets and the voice of the Global South as this particular document has...This is a document of the Global South; this is a document of the developing countries which came together and spelt out their priorities. And India has been the spokesperson of all the Global South and spelt out their priorities in this document," said Kant.

More Power to Africa

The formal inclusion of the AU as the 21st permanent member of the G20 has decisively transformed the character of the grouping, making it more inclusive and representative of the tectonic shift of economic power from the West to the rest. India, along with fraternal G20 countries of the Global South, played a major role in the AU's inclusion in the G20. This strategic move will ensure that African interests and priorities are reflected in the deliberations and outcomes of G20 summits and meetings in the future.

Climate Action and Green Growth

The New Delhi summit marked an important inflection point for global efforts to curb global warming by raising the targets for climate finance. There was significant progress as developed countries decided to walk the talk and expressed their willingness to fulfil their commitment of $ 100 billion for climate finance for the first time. The launch of the Global Biofuel Alliance on the sidelines of the New Delhi summit is expected to accelerate global efforts to meet net zero emission targets by facilitating trade in biofuels derived from various sources, including plant and animal wastes.

Developing countries of the Global South, which suffer the most from the damaging consequences of climate change, will benefit greatly from the G20's focus on green growth and sustainable development. According to the World Meteorological Organization, Africa suffers disproportionately from the climate crisis, despite being responsible for only a fraction of emissions. The climate emergency is harming food security, ecosystems and economies of nations in the continent. Climate change and environmental-related risks figure high on the World Economic Forum's Global Risks Report 2023, taking up six of the top ten biggest risks perceived to the world over the next decade. "As African and other developing economy countries, we face the task of meeting our climate commitments in the midst of significant developmental challenges like poverty, inequality and unemployment," said South Africa president Cyril Ramaphosa on X. "Climate change, environmental degradation, unsustainable consumption and production and resource scarcity are challenges that can only be addressed collectively and with a great deal of solidarity."

Reforming UN and Global Governance

At the New Delhi summit, Prime Minister Narendra Modi pitched strongly for the expansion of the UN Security Council and reforms in all global institutions to reflect the world's 'new realities.' Brazilian President Luiz Inácio Lula da Silva, who took over the G20 presidency from PM Modi, backed global governance reforms, saying the UNSC needs new developing countries as permanent and non-permanent members to regain political strength and greater representation for emerging countries at the World Bank and the IMF. The G20 summit in Delhi, with a strong focus on the Global South, has generated additional momentum for the reform of global governance institutions. The 55-nation AU's inclusion in G20 is going to accelerate reforms of the UN Security Council, global institutions and financial institutions.

According to Jakkie Cilliers, Chair of the Board and Head of African Futures & Innovation, Institute for Security Studies (South Africa), Africans have long rightly called for more representation in global economic and political governance. "Added African representation within BRICS+ and AU membership in the G20+ helps redress these deficits. It allows the continent to voice the need for much more important global governance reforms, namely, of the global financial architecture and the UN Security Council, and to agitate in the face of climate change for the prioritization of developmental issues from the perspective of the poorest and most marginalized region globally."

Bigger and Better MDBs

In many ways, the G20, with an almost equal number of developed and developing countries, is ideally placed to accelerate the multilateral reform process. In particular, given its provenance and focus on the global economy, the G20 can be the best forum for pushing reform of financial and economic multilateral institutions. Strengthening the Multilateral Development Banks (MDBs) to address shared global challenges of the 21st century was one of the key achievements of India's G20 presidency. In this regard, the agreement on the need for better, bigger, and more effective MDBs, as highlighted by India's Finance Minister Nirmala Sitharaman was a major takeaway. "It is so necessary to have better, bigger, and more effective MDBs because the developmental demands from all across the globe is so high; these institutions will have to be better and bigger," said Sitharaman. "This is also going to contribute to enhancing representation and voice of developing countries in the decision-making," she added. In pushing the reform of global governance, leaving no one behind has been India's guiding ethos. "We should ensure that no one is left behind in our pursuit of global solutions. So, we have endeavoured to support countries, especially those from the Global South, to be an integral part of the global decision-making process," said Sitharaman.

Bridging the North-South Divide

The overarching message that emanated from India's G20 presidency and the New Delhi summit was that given the enormity and complexity of global challenges the entire world, including developed and developing, should come together and act in the spirit of 'One Earth, One World One Future,' the anthem of India's G20 presidency.

Acting in silos is not an option. In its G20 presidency, and in its larger diplomatic outreach, India is not promoting an exclusivist South agenda, implying adversarial relations between the North and the South, but is focusing on building bridges between the Global North and the Global South. India's G20 presidency has strengthened the G20's role as an effective platform for managing North-South relations and bringing them together to address issues and challenges ranging from food, fuel and fertiliser crises to climate change, geopolitical conflicts and reform of global governance institutions.

Prime Minister Modi summed up the essence of India's syncretic approach at the concluding leaders session of the second Voice of Global South Summit on 17 November 2023. "We will all work towards One

Future with the spirit of '*Sabka Saath, Sabka Vikas, Sabka Vishwas*, and *Sabka Prayas*'. We will endeavour that no one is left behind in the Global South, where two-thirds of humanity lives. We will try to reduce the distance between North-South and East-West," he told the leaders of the Global South at the virtual summit. In this speech, he outlined the ten shared priorities of the Global South. These shared priorities, among other things, included removing poverty; climate action, climate justice, shared obligations and shared capacities; promoting a clean, sustainable, just, affordable and inclusive energy transition; addressing the challenges of food security; and prioritization of development finance to prevent the countries of the Global South from getting caught in the debt trap.

The other key shared priorities include leveraging digital public goods to improve the delivery of public services in the Global South, promoting inclusive multilateralism, representative global governance systems, promoting women-led development, connecting the Global South to the global value chains, bolstering cooperation against terrorism and extremism and full and timely implementation of the 2030 SDG Agenda. These ten steps have been endorsed and welcomed by the leaders of the Global South who participated in the two editions of the Voice of the Global South summit hosted by India during its G20 presidency. Going forward, this common South agenda should be carried forward by successive G20 presidencies and other multilateral forums. There is also a compelling case for institutionalizing the Voice of Global South Summit which should be held by all countries holding the G20 presidency in the future.

The Road Ahead

Building on the substantive achievements of India's G20 presidency in mainstreaming the priorities and interests of the Global South, Brazil, which currently dons the G20 mantle, is advancing the South agenda with added vigour, thereby ensuring that the interests of the developing countries figure high in meetings and discussions leading to the G20 summit in Rio de Janeiro in November 2024. In this regard, Brazil's President Luiz Inacio Lula da Silva argued eloquently for giving the Global South a larger voice in world decision-making at the meeting of the G20 foreign ministers in Rio de Janeiro on 27 February 2024. This push for accelerating global governance reforms was re-articulated vigorously at the G20 finance ministers' meeting in Sao Paulo. The Brazilian leader made a spirited case for better representation of the Global South in the multilateral system, including financial institutions set up after World War Two: the International Monetary Fund and the World Bank. "There are those who question the concept of the Global South, saying that we are too diverse to fit together. But many more interests unite us than differences that separate us," President Lula said.

This mainstreaming of the interests of the Global is finding greater traction and relevance in the developed world. "Brazil has focused on the interests and concerns of the so-called Global South. It is no longer a dialogue just between the great powers," EU foreign policy chief Josep Borrell said in an interview. "Having the African Union at the table is very important. In 20 years, one in four people in the world will be African," Borrell said. The United Nations has welcomed the move to induct the African Union in the G20 as the 55-nation grouping has a combined GDP of $ 3 trillion and a population of 1.4 billion.

The rise of the Global South, as epitomised in the induction of the AU in the G20, is part of what UN Secretary-General António Guterres described as 'inclusive, networked multilateralism' at the UNGA meeting marking the seventy-fifth anniversary of the United Nations in 2020. The rise of the Global South is also accelerating economic and political decentralization to world affairs. Rebeca Grynspan, Secretary-General at the United Nations Conference on Trade and Development (UNCTAD), has captured this defining transition as a movement from "hyper globalization to something that we are calling 'poly-globalization', which is more decentralized, with several centres and peripheries."

Going forward, one can expect the G20 countries to inject new ideas and initiatives in this onward march of the Global South, which has acquired an unstoppable momentum. India's External Affairs Minister Dr. S. Jaishankar has succinctly summed up India's G20 legacy in "relentlessly shining the spotlight on concerns of the Global South," in his book, '*Why Bharat Matters.*' "India's G20 presidency is also instructive in offering insights about how to navigate current world politics. By relentlessly shining the spotlight on concerns of the Global South, we were able to ensure that the G20 returned to its basic mandate of promoting international growth and development. Defining priorities in that regard and devising collective solutions were also objectives that were attained to a collective measure. Faced with the parallel challenges of East-West polarisation and North-South divide, each was utilised to mitigate the other problem," writes Dr. Jaishankar.

REFERENCES

Chand Manish. 2023. "Brazil will build on the legacy of India's G20 presidency". *India Writes Network*. 2 October 2023. https://www.indiawrites.org/india-and-the-world/india-g20-presidency-brazil-g20-brazil-g20-presidency-lula-visit-to-india-brazil-india-relations/

Chand Manish. 2023. "India's G20 moment: Forging a human-centric world order". *Daily Guardian*. 9 September 2023. https://thedailyguardian.com/indias-g20-moment-forging-a-human-centric-world-order/

Ero Comfort. 2024. "The Trouble With the Global South: What the West Gets Wrong About the Rest". (*Foreign Affairs,* 103, No. 2. 1 April 2024. https://www.foreignaffairs.com/world/trouble-global-south?utm_medium

Global Memo. 2023. "Was the G20 Summit a Turning Point for the Global South?". *Council of Councils*. 14 September 2023. (https://www.cfr.org/councilofcouncils/global-memos/was-g20-summit-turning-point-global-south)

Jaishankar S. 2024. *Why Bharat Matters*. New Delhi: Rupa Publications.

Lacey Simon. 2024. "What's the state of global trade? Here's what we learned in Davos". *World Economic Forum*. 25 January 2024. https://www.weforum.org/agenda/2024/01/the-state-of-global-trade/

Global South: Shaping Global Governance

ANIL WADHWA

The baton of the G20 presidency was passed on to India for a year on 1 December 2022. The previous 17 presidencies of the G20, which together represent 4.6 billion people, 85 per cent of the global GDP, 78 per cent of the world trade and 90 per cent of patents have delivered important results in relieving debt burdens, rationalising international taxation, capital and liquidity requirements for banks, recapitalisation of the IMF, stabilising the financial situation during the 2008 global financial crisis, creating a debt service suspension initiative, ensuring overall macroeconomic stability, and, at Bali, tackling multidimensional crises around water, climate change, food and energy security and recovery from the pandemic. Over the years, the G20 has also worked to widen its agenda to include issues like corruption, terror financing, jobs and social security, drug trafficking, migration, agriculture and food security, and health and climate change. India managed to build on these achievements but also delivered an inclusive, ambitious and action-oriented presidency. The world continues to face a geopolitical crisis due to conflicts in Ukraine, Gaza and the wider Middle East. There is the challenge of global breakdowns in supply chains, the crisis of climate finance and climate action, and many countries still face a debt crisis.

The UN Security Council has seen gridlocks due to geopolitics. China dominates in many as 15 of the world's multilateral institutions in a strategic and calculated takeover; the UN system badly needs reforms, and the G7 is perceived as an elitist, rich country grouping. Against this backdrop, the

G20 is seen as a promising forum with the right mix of industrialised and developing economies and more representative of the current global balance of power and influence. As the world's largest democracy, the fifth-largest economy, and the second most populous nation in the world, India has pursued a policy of strategic autonomy in recent times, and has the heft and credibility to act as a consensus maker. Prime Minister Modi stated on the eve of India taking over the presidency that India had some notable achievements to its credit, including the scalability of digital technologies, collective decision-making and democracy, a governance model of taking care of the marginalised while nurturing the creative genius of youth, and making national development a citizen-led 'people's movement'. India is successfully leveraging technology to create digital public goods that are open, inclusive and interoperable which has delivered revolutionary progress in social protection, health insurance, vaccination and tracking, financial inclusion, and electronic payments. It is the only country in G20 which is well on track to achieve its nationally determined goals for climate mitigation under the Paris Agreement. PM Modi has launched the LiFE (Lifestyle for Environment) movement in India making the adoption of successful lifestyles a mass movement. These proved to be useful templates, as India's G20 priorities were shaped in consultation with not only the G20 partners but also its fellow travellers in the Global South, whose voice often goes unheard. India hosted the most inclusive G20 meetings with delegates from 19 countries and the European Union plus over 800 special invitees from Bangladesh, Egypt, Nigeria, Oman, Singapore, Mauritius, the Netherlands, Spain and the UAE, and many international bodies and business leaders who attended the 200 meetings in 55 cities over the year.

Human-centric Globalisation

India had already outlined a vision of shaping a new paradigm of human-centric globalisation. According to Prime Minister Modi, this was to be achieved by encouraging sustainable and environment-friendly lifestyles, depoliticising the global supply of food, fertilisers and medical products in order to avoid humanitarian crises, and encourage an honest conversation on mitigating risks posed by weapons of mass destruction, which will contribute to global security. However, most importantly, India emphasised the role of technology in deciding India's geopolitical positioning as it would play a key role in striking technological and strategic alliances in a multi-polar world.

As Prime Minister Modi had said, all living beings and inanimate objects are composed of the five basic elements of earth, water, fire, air and space. India's G20 presidency promoted this universal sense of oneness; hence the theme 'One Earth, One Family, One Future', which, in turn, is based on the Vedantic doctrine of '*Vasudhaiva Kutumbakam*' – the world is one family. India had identified some priority issues – growth and prosperity, resilient global supply chains, small and medium enterprises, logistics, reforms in multilateral institutions like WTO, IMF and World Bank and women-led development under its G20 presidency. India took the lead in setting up new initiatives on disaster risk and resilience and Start Up 20.

India proposed a common digital platform for ease of cross-border trade, a legal aid system for developing countries for dispute settlement in WTO, ways to eliminate non-tariff measures that distort developing countries and LDCs, and a framework to address crucial issues at the WTO in clearly defined circumstances like the COVID-19 pandemic. Establishing an online digital portal that offers integrated trade and business information for market research by MSMEs was another proposal. India proposed the evolution of common principles to facilitate decentralised trading, an inclusive trade action plan that defines clear objectives for driving inclusion in the goods and services trade, and evolving principles to ensure food security through remunerative prices of farm goods. Geospatial mapping of the global value chains for critical and essential sectors, network restructuring, supply chain management solutions and building awareness of the risks of acute supply chain disruptions were other priority.

India played a critical role in ensuring global health security and the production and distribution of vaccines and can act as a credible voice of the developing world on the issue of food security, sustainable development goals and climate finance. It took the lead in the WTO with South Africa for a waiver from intellectual property protection of COVID-19-related medical technologies as well as related equipment.

In Africa and Latin America, and more widely in the Global South, there has been a lot of interest in the digitally enabled delivery platforms developed by India, which has shown that social security is not just a wealthy society's prerogative, by distributing free food grains to 800 million poor and direct benefit transfer to 450 million beneficiaries. Citizens of most developing countries do not have any kind of digital identity. Almost 2 billion people do not have bank accounts and around 130 countries do not have fast payment mechanisms. India's experience has shown that if digital architecture is made widely accessible, it can bring about socio-economic transformation. The use of digital technologies, if used judiciously, can become a force multiplier in the fight against poverty. India's success with the Unified Payments Interface (UPI), Direct Benefits Transfer and Aadhaar authentication in welfare schemes has a growing relevance for the developing world. The use of the CoWIN platform has enhanced vaccine accessibility and equity. Digital India is a technological model for global solutions of development and welfare at a low cost, which, in turn, will facilitate growth. The principle of 'data for development' was therefore an integral part of the overall theme of India's tenure. Under its presidency, India was determined to create mechanisms that strengthen the capacity of developing countries to tackle health crises such as the COVID-19 pandemic. India sought to work with the developing world to create a holistic, global health architecture that can respond better to future health crises. New approaches are needed to intellectual property, innovation and co-development of health technology to ensure a more inclusive response to health crises. India's focus was on the benefits that technological progress and evidence-based policy can provide when it comes to expanding access to health.

The G20 Summit under India's presidency in 2023 will be remembered for the shaping of the G20 as a much more dynamic platform, and for putting the so-called Global South squarely at the centre of the global governance agenda. In the process, the Global South also underscored its own credentials as a player willing and able to shape global outcomes rather than being a passive recipient of decisions taken by others. By organising two important 'Voice of the Global South Summits' on 12-13 January and on 17 November 2023 – one prior to the G20 presidency and one as a follow-up, India managed to live up to its role as a responsible global stakeholder and as a leader of the Global South. The convening of another summit to discuss issues related to artificial intelligence and its impact on the Global South was clearly indicative of the creation of a new institutional platform for sustaining solidarity with the developing world. In fact, the opportunity to host the G20 Summit was the trigger for India to build on its reputation.

Voice of Global South Summit

The simple purpose of the voice of the Global South Summit was to ascertain the key concerns and needs of developing countries that could be taken up and pursued by the G20 presidency during India's tenure from December 2022 to November 2023. The inclusive programmes and the opportunity for 125 countries to articulate their views received considerable appreciation. The most tangible outcome was that the host obtained rich inputs that later moulded the G20 agenda.

The G20 Summit and the consensus on a New Delhi Declaration reminded us that there is a world beyond the major powers, which is also seeking a role in global decision-making. Changes in sustainable development, inclusive growth, climate change, food security, digital divide, emerging tech regulation, and multilateral development bank reform cannot be undertaken without the developing world at the table. The inclusion of the African Union (AU) in the G20 has fundamentally altered the character of the platform, making it more inclusive and representative of the emerging global order. From an African perspective, the double standards of organisations such as the G20 and G7 are legion, including rhetoric on vaccines, debt sustainability, and development finance not matched by implementation. For the Global South, where demands for global support to overcome poverty, fragility, and catastrophes are the highest, the possibilities of G20-driven benefits are always going to depend on the leverage exerted by emerging economies like India. It is in this context that the priority issues and targets from the summit in India – the need for more inclusive growth, accelerated implementation of the sustainable development goals, accelerated action to mitigate climate change adversities, health emergencies, debt vulnerabilities, reform of multilateral development banks, and strengthening more equitable multilateral bodies, among others

– are indications that show that increased participation and the voice of the Global South can change the agenda of global action and partnership.

The second voice of the Global South Summit in India in November 2023 focused on the Global South getting together for a common future. The essential purpose was twofold: to apprise high-level representatives of the Global South with the deliberations and outcomes of the G20 Summit, and to ensure that momentum is sustained with the support of developing countries for optimal implementation of the G20 decisions. India inaugurated the Global South Centre for Excellence, to be called DAKSHIN, an acronym for Development and Knowledge Sharing Initiative. It will serve as a think tank and a repository of knowledge and development initiatives that promote greater collaboration among developing nations. Ministerial sessions went into a whole gamut of India's G20 priorities ranging from sustainable development goals, energy transition, climate action finance, digital transformation, debt relief, women-led development, counter-terrorism, and reform of the Security Council. The admission of the AU and the role of India was widely appreciated.

The Road Ahead

In sum, there were three important takeaways from the second voice of the Global South Summit: First, the Global South orientation of the G20 Summit was fully noted because over 50 per cent of the content of the G20 New Delhi Leaders Declaration is related exclusively to the needs of the Global South. Second, there was recognition that the success in securing a seat for the AU in G20 demonstrated that global groupings can be persuaded to respond to the changing global realities in an inclusive fashion. Third, that resolving global challenges required not confrontation but a mix of cooperation, consultation and coordination.

The mission to further the cause of the Global South, however, has a long road ahead. This mission will be truly accomplished when implementation of the G20 decisions gets underway and picks up momentum. For this, the Global South nations have to keep their collective voices robust. The rise and voice of the Global South is becoming strident. Brazil is hosting the 2024 G20 Summit, and South Africa the year after that. Even though the Global South is not united on most matters, its countries do nurse a deepening frustration with the current system that keeps them down.

India today is keen to provide solutions to global challenges, announcing plans for a global biofuels alliance and India-Middle East-Europe connectivity partnership as well as its willingness to share its own success in digital public infrastructure. The current international financial institutions will need to be restructured to conform to the new realities of climate change and bring in new instruments like blended finance, first class guarantees and credit enhancement to allow private capital to flow into the Global South. India will have to work with the Global South countries to ensure free trade and resist protectionism. Climate change actions will require climate finance, which is critical along with energy transition.

Regionally, India has renewed its focus on the 14-member FIPIC – the Forum for India-Pacific Islands Cooperation, launched in 2014. At the last FIPIC summit held in Port Moresby, India promised several bilateral projects in the fields of IT, healthcare, climate change, food supply, and medicines, among others. India unveiled a 12-point programme, which includes the promise to build a hospital, extend scholarships, dialysis centres, and subsidised medicines. India has continued its developmental cooperation with countries of the ASEAN in diverse fields through a bilateral cooperation fund, a science and technology fund and a green fund. It has also extended a $1 billion line of credit for connectivity projects.

In Africa, India has positioned itself as a partner in development, has extended concessional loans of over $ 12.3 billion, and allocated $ 700 million in grand assistance. Its capacity-building initiatives are focused on skills, technology and knowledge transfer. Over half of the India-led International Solar Alliance members are from Africa. In the 2022-23 budget, India has allocated 45 lines of credit worth $ 14.5 billion covering 263 projects to seven countries in India's neighbourhood, namely, Bangladesh, Nepal, Sri Lanka, Myanmar, the Maldives, Mauritius, and Seychelles. The projects cover sectors like roads, railways, power, ports and shipping, telecom, health, education and aviation.

India is also part of the QUAD, which has taken several initiatives for development cooperation in the Indo-Pacific, in climate change, new and emerging technologies, vaccines and health, and is now seen as an enabler to harmonise domestic structural reforms with a secure and enabling external environment of trade, investment, technology, and capital flows.

For India, the next challenge as a leader of the Global South is to ensure maximum coordination with Brazil and South Africa as the next two presidents of G20. Through close engagement, deft diplomacy, and respecting the sensitivities of its G20 successors, India can continue serving the cause of the Global South constructively. India has emerged from its G20 presidency as a global agenda setter, a driver of inclusive global growth for global good, and a constructive consensus maker. The well-developed and efficiently functional Development Promotion Programmes of India in Africa and Asia, the Pacific as well as Latin America including ITEC which enhances education, skilling and specialisation, can be used to promote a South-South Agenda and create constituencies for India in these countries. The lines of credit can be focused on progressing the G20 agenda for common development. However, for all this to come together and succeed, India will need to ensure that the government, business, academia, educational institutions, opinion makers, media and the public at large work in unison. India's presidency represented the most vulnerable in the world and has enhanced inclusivity and intra-South economic integration.

17

African Union's Effective Participation in the G20

PRADEEP S. MEHTA

In a landmark achievement for India's G20 presidency, the African Union (AU) was granted a permanent seat at the G20 at its summit in New Delhi in September 2023. This significant gesture recognised the individual and collective aspirations of 54 African countries for their greater and more effective presence on the global stage.

The G20 is the international forum bringing together the 20 largest and fastest-growing economies. Its members account for more than 80 per cent of the world's GDP (Gross Domestic Product), 75 per cent of global trade and 60 per cent of the population.

Mainstreaming Africa

The inclusion of the AU into this body reflects the ethos that India has propounded during its G20 presidency – *Vasudhaiva Kutumbakam* – the World is One Family. In this context, it is important to understand that while the old-school multilateralism is waning, the G20 has emerged as a (perhaps the) premier forum for deliberations among the global leadership on challenges that the world is facing.

Moreover, following the COVID-19 pandemic, it is evident that the world order did not remain the same and should not be so. A shift from a GDP-centric view of the world to a human-centric view was felt; resilience and reliability in the global supply chain had grown in importance and the reform of global institutions were needed to boost multilateralism in an emerging avatar. It is in this context that Prime Minister Modi advocated the importance of mainstreaming the marginalised aspirations of developing countries, the Global South and Africa.[1]

> "It was in the spirit of 'Sabka Saath' that India proposed permanent membership for the African Union in the G20. I believe that we all agree on this proposal," said Prime Minister Modi, as he invited the AU Chair to the high table.

Though Africa has been advocating for a full membership of the G20 for the past seven years, it was Prime Minister Modi who wrote to all G20 leaders in June 2023 seeking a permanent membership for the 55-nation AU. This group is home to some of the fast-growing economies in the world and has a combined GDP of $ 2.4 trillion. US President Joe Biden had already expressed his support for the African Union's permanent membership in the G20 at the US-Africa Leaders' Summit in December 2022.[2]

The AU, as a successor to the Organisation of African Unity (OAU), was officially launched in June 2002 to focus on an increased integration of African states to drive Africa's growth and economic development and enable Africa to play its rightful role in the global economy. At the same time, addressing multifaceted social, economic and political problems compounded as they were by negative aspects of globalisation.[3]

Africa's development agenda is guided by the AU's Agenda 2063. It is a strategic framework that aims to deliver on its goal for inclusive and sustainable development, and is a manifestation of the pan-African drive for unity, self-determination, freedom, progress and collective prosperity. Its focus areas are as follows:

- Sustainable and inclusive economic growth that reduces poverty and increases income level, equality and decent jobs,
- Value addition in agricultural products and growth in agri-business and industries,
- Manufacturing-based industrialisation,
- Human capital development, skills revolution in science and technology and innovation, gender development, youth

empowerment and employment generation for youth and women,
- Social security and protection for all people,
- Infrastructural development,
- Good governance supported by capable institutions, and
- Promotion of culture, arts and sports, peace and security.[4]

Among other positives, the AU brings to the G20 a continent that boasts the world's largest free trade area. The African Continental Free Trade Area (AfCFTA) came into force in January 2021, with the objective of increasing intra-African trade and investment through deeper levels of trade liberalisation and enhanced regulatory harmonisation and coordination.

Why Africa Matters

Africa as a full member of the G20 significantly boosts the number of economies represented in this body, which, in turn, represents 100 countries in the form of 19 independent countries and 82 European and African countries. Most importantly, 60 per cent of the world's renewable energy resources and over 30 per cent of the minerals that are crucial for renewable and low-carbon technologies lie in the African continent.

According to a recent United Nations report on Africa's economic development, the Democratic Republic of Congo alone possesses nearly half the world's cobalt, a crucial metal for lithium-ion batteries.

The continent also possesses the necessary resources to combat Climate Change, which affects Africa the most, in spite of contributing the least to this challenge.[5] Africa will account for over half of the world's projected population growth of 1.7 billion people in 2050, comprising a young workforce with a median age of 18 years, a growing consumer base and rising disposable incomes.[6]

Advantage India

Africa gaining membership of the G20 under India's presidency presents significant political and diplomatic gains to India. It buttresses India's status as a key player in global governance and a country which champions inclusivity and diversity on the international stage. This is also in line with India's global aspiration to foster a multipolar world with strategic autonomy and its desire for a shift in the world order by being more inclusive.

Throughout its presidency of the G20, India shared a vision of being the voice of the Global South. India has been raising issues concerning the Global South countries in international forums and at the United Nations meetings and conferences. At the very beginning of its G20 presidency, India hosted the Voice of Global South Summit virtually with representatives from 125 countries. At the G7 Summit also, India ensured that the Global South remained centre stage.[7]

Prime Minister Modi's move towards the AU will give India more weight within the G20, given its geopolitical influence and booming economy. Backing the AU is evidence of India voicing not only for the Global South but also signifies a natural progression and cooperation between India and Africa as a whole. In this context, it is important to note that there is a large Indian Diaspora in most African countries which has invested a huge amount of capital and created many jobs. It can be strategically mobilised to support Indian interests.

Since the forward-looking regime of Prime Minister Narendra Modi, India's image has become a matter of pride to the Indian Diaspora all over. This is a critical intangible to explore in pursuing the India-Africa relationship.

Neo-Scramble for Africa

Furthermore, it is important to underline that Africa for many years has been a playground for major powers like the USA, Russia, China and the European countries, all competing for political and economic influence in the resource-rich continent.

Russia, though occupied with the Ukraine war, remains actively involved in African politics through proxies.[8] Europe, grappling with rising migration from Africa and the Middle East, has also been noticed reinvigorating its relationships in the continent.

China already has created a strong and expanding foothold in Africa. It first reached the continent in 2000 and since the formation of the Forum on China Africa Cooperation (FOCAC) it has come a long way indicating evolving Chinese interests in the African continent. Among other initiatives, China has been aggressively pursuing its own economic interests in this resource-rich continent through investments in infrastructure and mining under the Belt and Road Initiative.[9] It has helped African countries develop healthcare, trade and infrastructure but also emerging industries such as the digital economy, green industry and vocational education.

The cooperation between China and Africa is expected to grow closer and expand to other sectors. According to the China-Africa Cooperation Vision 2035, China-Africa annual trade is expected to reach $ 300 billion in 2035. It will also invest $ 60 billion in Africa by 2035 in support of African agriculture, manufacturing, infrastructure, environmental protection, digital economy and blue economy.[10]

Therefore, given all these developments and the strategic autonomy that India follows in pursuing its foreign policy, Africa's G20 membership could be a huge opportunity to boost India's influence in Africa and balance the Chinese influence to the best extent possible.

India's outreach to Africa began long back with Mahatma Gandhi fighting against colonial oppression and apartheid in South Africa (the only G20 member from Africa until now) and subsequently leading India's struggle for independence during the early 1900s. Nelson Mandela was inspired by Gandhi's ideals in his struggles against apartheid. After India attained its independence in 1947, it raised its voice for African liberation, taking their case to all international forums available at the time. The end of racial struggle and decolonisation became the rallying point of India-Africa relations. Through the Bandung Declaration of 1955, the Group of 77 and the Non-Aligned Movement (NAM), India attempted to be a champion of the interests of developing countries from Africa. This was revisited recently at Kampala, Uganda, in January 2024 when the 19th NAM Summit was held to reinforce its mandate.

India-Africa Engagement

In the freedom struggles of many African countries, India has played a significant role by voicing their concerns at international fora, including the UN and the Commonwealth Secretariat. It also provided political asylum to many of its leaders to escape imprisonment and persecution due to their freedom struggles. Even currently, many Africans visit India for higher studies, training and medical tourism. Thus, India has a huge amount of political goodwill among African countries.

In the last two decades, India's engagement with African countries has increased with a large number of public and private sector companies investing in Africa. India launched a duty-free tariff preferential scheme for Least Developed Countries (LDCs) in 2008 which benefitted 33 African states. Simultaneously, China and Brazil too launched similar preferential schemes. Multilateral engagement was launched with the first India-Africa Forum Summit (IAFS) in 2008. Following this, the 2nd IAFS was held in Addis Ababa in 2011 and the 3rd was held in New Delhi in 2015. The 4th IAFS is likely to be held in 2024, perhaps in Africa.

The Ministry of External Affairs also runs the Indian Technical and Economic Cooperation Programme (ITEC) since 1964. It is one of the oldest institutionalised arrangements for international capacity building having trained more than 200,000 officials from 160-plus countries in both civilian and defence sectors. Under this programme and recommendations of IAFS, India has also provided support to establish research and training institutes in Africa in various sectors. The investment made by India in the ITEC programme totals more than $ 2 bn until now, most of which has been deployed in Africa.

Other than direct support, India has also entered into agreements with Japan, the USA, France, Germany, the UK, etc., to provide trilateral development aid to African countries. In this model, the rich country provides the funding and India provides appropriate technology and supervision to implement projects at costs lower than what the rich countries would have had to pay if they were to implement them themselves.

Furthermore, India has been investing directly in several economic areas in Africa, namely in the ICT sector. It invested $ 100 million in the Pan-African E-Network to bridge the digital divide in Africa, leveraging its strengths in information technology. It set up a fibre optic network to provide satellite connectivity, tele-medicine and tele-education to countries of Africa. The e-Vidya Bharti and e-Arogya Bharti (e-VBAB) introduced in 2019, focused on providing free tele-education to African students and continued medical education for healthcare professionals. Overall, India has made a commitment to the world to roll out its successful Digital Public Infrastructure throughout. It has already covered nearly 18 countries.

Indian pharmaceutical companies have provided affordable generic medicines to African countries, contributing to improved healthcare access. India is known as the pharma factory of the world. She has also deployed medical teams and offered technical assistance to combat diseases like HIV/AIDS, malaria, and Ebola in the Global South.

India has contributed significantly in the area of defence as well. It signed an MoU with all African nations on the Indian Ocean Rim (IOR) to boost defence cooperation. India has hosted two India-Africa Defence Dialogues (IADD) at the defence ministers' level, on the sidelines of the Defence Expo at Lucknow (2020) and Gandhinagar (2022). It is engaged in the training of military officials from African countries in India and in Africa.

In 2022, India started the first edition of the Trilateral Maritime Exercise with Tanzania and Mozambique to enhance maritime cooperation in the region. Presently India is building a military base on Agalega, an island belonging to Mauritius, to enable a defence and peace keeping post in the African and Indian Ocean Region. Furthermore, India has provided the highest number of UN-led peace keeping forces in strife-torn African countries.

In terms of future engagement on G20 issues, the 2025 G20 Summit will be held in South Africa. Considering the close relations between both countries and the presence of a large Indian Diaspora, further progress in India's constructive engagement in Africa through this platform is likely to expand substantially.

NOTES

1. 'Human-Centric Globalisation: Taking India G20 to the last mile, leaving none behind' by Narendra Modi, Prime Minister of India, *The New Indian Express*, 31 October 2023, available at https://www.newindianexpress.com/nation/2023/sep/07/human-centric-globalisation-taking-g20-to-the-last-mile-leaving-none-behind-2612617.html
2. https://www.reuters.com/world/us-provide-165-million-support-elections-governance-africa-2022-12-15/
3. Au.int.
4. https://au.int/en/agenda2063/overview

5. https://bfsi.economictimes.indiatimes.com/news/industry/african-union-becomes-permanent-member-of-g20-all-you-need-to-know-about-it

6, It's time for Africa, https://www.ciiblog.in/a-time-for-africa

7. https://economictimes.indiatimes.com/news/india/g20-how-india-emerged-as-the-voice-of-global-south/articleshow/103410416.cms

8. https://carnegieendowment.org/2023/02/28/russia-s-growing-footprint-in-africa-s-sahel-region-pub-89135

9. China's massive Belt and Road Initiative, https://www.cfr.org/backgrounder/chinas-massive-belt-and-road-initiative

10. https://news.cgtn.com/news/2023-06-30/China-injects-fresh-momentum-into-Africa-s-infrastructure-boom-1l3Xe17Y4es/index.html#:~:text=China%20injects%20fresh%20momentum%20into%20Africa's%20infrastructure%20boom%20%2D%20CGTN&text=China%20is%20helping%20African%20countries,and%20technologies%20to%20the%20continent.

18

The African Continent: A Voice, an Opportunity, and a Greater Role

PAMLA GOPAUL, KENNEDY MBEVA AND REUBEN MAKOMERE

An emergent Africa necessitates a greater role in global governance. The African Union's induction into the G20 as a full member is a defining step to reshape a crucial global governance institution to make it more appropriate for a world with multiple crises. It is a step in the right direction that the important great and major powers expressed support for Africa's candidacy.

From the impact of the COVID-19 pandemic to debt crises and climate change, African countries are facing significant development challenges due to global problems for which they are least responsible. But Africa is also a frontier in innovative governance, especially as epitomised by the conclusion and ratification of the African Continental Free Trade Agreement (AfCFTA), in which 46 of the 54 signatories (85.2 %) have deposited their instruments of AfCFTA ratification which illustrates Africa's divergent globalisation against the tide of deglobalisation. Africa, therefore, has a prominent role to play in governing the emerging poly-crisis world order. Having a seat at the G20 is not only the right thing to do, but also a wise move in reshaping global governance and reinvigorating cooperation between Africa and the rest of the world in a fast-changing geopolitical and economic landscape.

Three fundamental shifts justify Africa's membership in the G20. First, the unfolding poly-crisis in the economic, ecological, and security realms are posing significant challenges to global governance. Hegemonic leadership, where a few powerful countries provide critical public goods, is no longer sufficient. Recent reports from the Inter-governmental Panel on Climate Change (IPCC), for instance, have highlighted the global socio-ecological risks posed by climate change. Additionally, the rapid yet uneven recovery from the pandemic has also highlighted significant economic vulnerabilities across Africa and the world. In a global economic system already weakened by shocks associated with the pandemic, Africa and other developing countries are already exposed to significant financial pressure due to the high cost of commodities including fuel, food, and borrowings (United Nations Conference on Trade and Development, UNCTAD, 2022). As further illustration of these risks, the International Monetary Fund (IMF) and the World Bank identified up to 16 low-income African countries as states at high risk of debt distress, while seven were already in debt distress.

Age of Poly-Crisis

Global security and geopolitical challenges are illustrative of the increasingly complex suite of challenges facing multilateral governance institutions. High commodity prices arising out of the war in Ukraine and associated disruptions in the supply chains of critical products such as grain, fertilisers, and energy provides an apt example of the multiple crises that face and influence global cooperation. In a region that plays a central role in the global supply of various products, both Russia and Ukraine provide approximately 30 per cent of the world exports of wheat, as well as 20 per cent of maize and over 50 per cent of sunflower oil. Additionally, Russia and neighbouring Belarus provide about 20 per cent of global fertiliser exports. The war, associated disruptions, and attendant economic sanctions have resulted in severe restrictions on the supply of these commodities to Africa and other parts of the world thus resulting in an increase in trade costs. The shortfall in wheat supplies from Russia and Ukraine has affected Africa particularly hard due to the heavy dependence for an outsized share of their wheat imports. In contrast with other more developed parts of the world such as the European Union, which could make up the shortfall by tapping into regional producers and/or other alternative sources, African states have often struggled to cope given the lack of alternative partners and global presence that can ensure the provision of additional imports.

Second, the ongoing rapid global power shifts are reconfiguring the global economy in significant ways, leading some commentators to talk of an emerging geoeconomic order. With the shift from unipolarity to a multipolar world, cooperation especially amongst the great powers is becoming more challenging. Moreover, emerging powers are establishing alternative institutions and forums for cooperation. These changes are not only occurring on a global scale but also present particularly unique challenges for the African continent and its engagement in global affairs. An expansion in the involvement of great powers including China, Russia, and the USA, in addition to intermediate powers such as Turkey and Saudi Arabia, for instance, epitomizes the changing global geopolitical landscape and its impact on Africa (Gustavo de Carvalho and Laura Rubidge, 2022). While this expansion of the geopolitical space has presented significant opportunities such as additional avenues for development financing, it has also brought about new complexities including navigating debt restructuring and achieving effective and equitable cooperation on contemporary problems such as climate change. The recent wave of high-profile visits to Africa by Western and non-Western delegations such as US Vice-President Kamala Harris, US Treasury Secretary Janet Yellen, Secretary of State Anthony Blinken, French President Emmanuel Macron, China's Foreign Minister Qin Gang, and Russian Minister of Foreign Affairs Sergey Lavrov, for instance, highlights the complicated strategic choices that the continent needs to make to navigate the increasing complexities associated with the changing geopolitical dynamics (Nuzulack Dausen, 2023; Mohammed Yusuf, 2023; Elizabeth Pineau, 2023; Reuters, 2023; US Department of State, 2023). Progressively, intense competition between China, the USA and powers such as the European Union (EU), United Kingdom (UK), India, Turkey, and Russia for greater influence across Africa are already having important reverberations across the continent's political and developmental landscape. While global powers have their goals and interests in Africa, there is an increasing demand for more complex approaches to regional and global governance that ensure that this rising interest does not diminish the continent's agency. It is gradually being recognised, for instance, that Africa's abundant natural resources could supplement Europe's need for alternatives to Russian gas, oil, and coal. Despite the increasingly vocal push for a just transition from fossil fuels, African states have the opportunity to maximise emerging opportunities to negotiate more favourable and equitable trade agreements as noted by Senegalese President Macky Sall. The geopolitical interest in Africa dovetails with its importance as the largest regional voting bloc at the United Nations (UN), making Africa an important player in international geopolitics.

Demographic Shift

Third, rapid demographic shifts are reshaping the global image. Given that one out of five people in the world in 2050 will be African, and two out of five babies will be born in Africa, how Africans envision the world is indispensable for redesigning global governance. Asymmetries in terms of governance, approaches and tools reduce the potential of the cooperation system to enable Africa's development and address the common challenges facing all countries. Africa's population, for instance, is projected to increase to about 2.8 billion by 2060, up from the current estimate of 1.4 billion (*statistictimes* n.d.). The population in the Eastern and Southern African regions alone is projected to increase to about 1.1 billion people by 2050 from approximately 633 million in 2021 (United Nations Population Fund, UNFPA, 2023). While this uptick presents significant opportunities to harness a demographic dividend and turbo charge rapid economic development necessary to transform the continent, it also poses significant challenges, especially for African policy makers particularly around pathways to address the specific and pressing developmental aspirations for current and future generations in the continent. Taken together, these three fundamental shifts provide important heuristics for the increasingly significant role that Africa can play in shaping global governance and reinvigorating multilateral cooperation in the age of poly-crisis. Crucially, these challenges have highlighted the widening gap between rising complex global problems, a rapidly changing geo-political landscape around which these problems are to be addressed, and the current capacity of conventional global governance institutions to cope with these problems. Enhanced engagement with the G20, beginning with a seat at the forum, would be an important step in realising a more meaningful and nimble form of multilateral cooperation to solve current and emerging global problems in a manner that not only offers important opportunities for both parties but is also more responsive and representative of the current global geopolitical landscape.

G20's Role in Africa

The G20 presents an important opportunity to explore and implement nimbler, fit-for-purpose cooperation frameworks to tackle current and emerging ecological, economic, and geopolitical challenges in a more equitable and responsive manner. Indeed, there have been several important initiatives within the G20 that are highly relevant to the African continent, especially in the context of realising the African Union Agenda 2063. The G20 Compact with Africa, for example, was meant to enhance the continent's attractiveness to private investment through technical and institutional improvements on existing macro, business, and financing frameworks (G20 Compact With Africa, n.d.). Since its launch in 2017 under the German G20 presidency, the initiative has attracted the interest of several African states including Benin, Côte d'Ivoire, Egypt, and Ethiopia. The G20 Debt Treatment beyond the Debt Service Suspension Initiative (DSSI) was another mechanism that was initiated at the height of the pandemic to help alleviate the financial pressure on low-income developing countries occasioned by servicing debt repayments in the middle of the pandemic (IMF, 2021). In this sense, low-income countries were temporarily allowed to suspend their debt payments till the end of 2021. In April 2021, the G20 developed the DSSI to facilitate debt restructuring negotiations as they pertain to low-income countries (William N. Kring, 2021). While considered largely ineffective, the initiatives were representative of the institutional agility that can be harnessed and leveraged to develop more meaningful forms of cooperation and address current and emerging challenges including the Just Energy Transition Partnerships (JTEPs), debt restructuring and pandemic response.

The case for strengthening Africa's engagement within the G20 should not be seen as a mere case of charitable benevolence but a long overdue partnership that is necessary if current and emerging global challenges are to be addressed. Significant economic and political relationships already exist between African countries and current G20 members. These relationships are likely to continue expanding in scope and importance in a multi-polar world characterised by poly-crisis. The increasingly active presence of global powers in the continent combined with the need to address complex current and emerging universal problems including climate change, debt restricting, and post-COVID recovery present additional justification for why a more representative, responsive G20 is needed. Excluding Africa from such platforms runs the risk of alienating a critical constituency at a time of great transformation in global governance and international politics.

Additionally, enhancing such cooperation arrangements is a significant step towards reforming and adapting to changing global realities. The G20 can support and enhance Africa's contribution to global (economic) governance in several ways including agenda-setting, legitimacy, policy coordination, and capacity building. By incorporating Africa's policy priorities into its core agenda, the G20 can ensure that the views of a significant global populace are incorporated into its governance activities. Born of a crisis, the G20's nimble structure allows it to respond to global crises quickly and effectively. It is also best suited to addressing complex challenges that may not neatly fit into a particular governance regime, such as the JTEPs and debt restructuring efforts. Strengthening engagement with Africa thus takes a normative component, especially in relation to increased legitimacy, and representation in addressing current and emerging problems. The African experience in relation to the COVID vaccines further highlighted the need to enhance equity, representation, and fairness, especially given the disparities in access to vaccines between the G20 countries and sub-Saharan African countries. The United Nations Children's Fund (UNICEF), for example, acknowledged in 2021 that G20 member-countries received up to 15 times more COVID-19 vaccine doses per capita compared to those in sub-Saharan Africa. Strengthening legitimacy amid such disparities is therefore not only necessary but an imperative for the creation of meaningful cooperative arrangements, especially for the G20. Crucial to generating legitimacy and equity is enhancing meaningful engagement with Africa through avenues such as more concrete membership in the G20. By design, the G20 is based on exclusive membership. While this limited membership can enable faster decision-making, many of the global challenges that fall within the mandate of the G20 require broader engagement, especially with countries and regions that bear a disproportionate impact of the challenges. Climate change, for instance, presents a particularly prescient example of this dynamic given that Africa is responsible for only around 3 per cent of global carbon emissions yet loses about 5 per cent to 15 per cent of GDP due to climate change (African Development Bank, 2022).

Recommendations to G20

Boost institutional connections: There are already many formal and informal institutional frameworks for the G20. African nations have created substantial institutional frameworks for coordinating concurrently through the AU. The first steps might involve coordinating the G20's and Africa's top priorities on a technical and policy level. Building blocks for these choices might be the ongoing partnership between the Think20 (T20) and the Policy Bridge Tank of the African Union Development Agency (AUDA-NEPAD). Such momentum could also be created through political and policy coordination.

Reforms and changes to policy: Aligning the G20 with Africa's major policy concerns would be a difficult political step, but one that is crucial. This would encourage synergy and make the areas of cooperation clearer. Importantly, while Africa and the G20 do not have to collaborate in every area, they can reach an understanding on political topics of shared concern. More particularly, this might entail harmonising some of the G20 and African Union Agenda 2063's fundamental principles. To create the necessary synergies to reach a consensus on policy problems of shared interest, it will be important to develop trust-building institutions, such as policy clearing houses and platforms for dialogue.

Rethinking cooperative models will lead to more equal engagement; Africa's engagement with the G20 must be meaningful and equitable. Participation alone will not be sufficient to achieve the expressive cooperation needed to address the ongoing and upcoming challenges facing Africa and the rest of the globe. For instance, how G20 collaboration with the African Union would affect higher education and research in Africa, how debt in African countries stifles public funding for education, how Africa has 25 per cent of the world's disease burden but only 4 of clinical trials globally due to research capacity, funding, and regional data, and many other examples.

Given that Africa is underrepresented in important global decision-making institutions and processes that go beyond post-war laws and principles, rethinking multilateral system governance to make it more representative is essential. Africa should have a place in the primary bodies where economic and financial decisions are made due to its population weight and cumulative GDP. Therefore, Africa should have a permanent seat in the G20 through the African Union, as requested by President Sall and backed in November and December 2022 by the Presidents of France, Japan, and the USA.

Africa Factor in India's G20 Presidency

GURJIT SINGH

India's successful implementation of its G20 presidency was as close to impeccable and unexpected as possible. A consensual Leaders Declaration and a consensus on admitting the African Union (AU) as a full member of the G20 were astonishing for their emergence, speed, and meticulousness. For both to occur on the first day itself surprised most analysts, many of whom predicted a Chair's Summary than a leader's statement.

A result of hard negotiations, these two decisions set the tone for discussions so that the G20 could truly be responsive to global requirements, particularly of the developing countries.

India's G20 presidency unfolded at a time when the world was wracked by big power rivalry. This has since got worse. It is marked by protectionism rising from the economic downturn, which followed the COVID-19 pandemic. Globalisation, which promised benefits for all, is tested. It was left to the emerging countries to speak up for globalisation consequent to the Ukraine crisis and the slow post-pandemic recovery. The breach of supply chains of energy, food and fertiliser were consequences of the Ukraine crisis and derailed the post-COVID recovery on which the developing countries were counting. Instead, the developing countries faced unprecedented onslaught on their economies, which had diverted substantial resources into dealing with the pandemic. The West Asia crisis has accentuated these problems, exacerbating insecurity and cost escalation which India warned against.

Issues like debt relief, public health, new supply chains that can withstand strategic differences, and greater dependence on resilient value chains among dependable countries came to the fore at the G20.

Prioritising the Global South

For some decades, the developing countries and the Global South have felt neglected by the international order. Besides the dominance of the Bretton Woods institutions, the creation of new China-led institutions like the New Development Bank and the AIIB did not assuage their concerns. The China-led BRI, which used the NDB and the AIIB, created problems of debt and a lack of imagination in planning projects. Thus, between the lending of the multilateral development banks (MDBs) and from China, the Global South was strangled and the pandemic accentuated that realisation.

In these institutions, the Global South had the opportunity to speak but was rarely heard, and often kept out of important decisions whether they be on climate finance, terrorism, migration, debt relief, or the maintenance of international peace and security. The international order was meant to empower countries and peoples; the way it operated it disempowered them further.

The G20 was the perfect opportunity for India to speak confidently about its pro-South agenda. It involved the Global South in full measure. First, its list of guest countries invited included Bangladesh, Egypt, Mauritius, the Netherlands, Nigeria, Oman, Singapore, Spain and the UAE. This preference for countries of the Global South that could play a role in their regions and contribute to the betterment of human destiny was evocative.

Secondly, in January 2023, through the virtual summit for the Voice of the Global South, India consulted 125 countries on a series of subjects. This engagement was not only at the level of leaders and foreign ministers, but through functional ministries. This consultative process for the first time brought almost every country of the Global South into the process of the G20, which otherwise was becoming restrictive. India's promise to its partners in the Global South has always been to work with them for a better place in the international order.

India has honed this process through its long-standing 75 years of engagement with countries of the Global South. Well before the Bandung Conference in 1955, India had engaged with the newly emerging countries. Subsequently, India was among the leadership of the nonaligned movement, the Group of 77 and, in the current century, had successful partnerships with Africa, the Caribbean, the Pacific, ASEAN and Central Asia.

The African Dimension

India addressed this re-prioritisation of the Global South in several ways. It knew it could run away with the G20 agenda. All members of the G20 being equal, and some having larger economic heft, wanted to direct the G20 as per their priorities. India succeeded in adjusting those priorities by adding those relevant to the Global South. This was a feature of India's G20 working groups and meetings held on different subjects before and during its presidency. This modulated the priorities through the G20 to realistic and preferred goals

Many countries in the Global South see India as a positive model for plural, democratic, development. They appreciate India's strategic autonomy, too. They believe they can emulate India. Its achievements during the pandemic and thereafter accentuated that respect. India posited them into the G20 process and offered examples of impactful development.

Leveraging these aspects, India took the initiative to have the African Union as a permanent member of the G20, rather than a frequent guest as was the case for several years. This was a courageous decision that brought Africa a seat at the high table and provided an influential forum to articulate its own concerns and priorities.

African Priorities

There are five important sectors among many thrust areas which India pursued to fulfil a larger and better vision for the G20. These are all directly relevant to African priorities.

The first is how to deal with debt stress. Strengthening multilateral development banks to be responsive to shared current global challenges, financing for resilient, inclusive and sustainable development, leveraging

Digital Public Infrastructure (DPI) for enhancing financial inclusion and productivity gains were among Indian priorities.

Secondly, the issue of climate finance is a major concern because repeated assurances to help developing countries are unfulfilled. The strategy to keep negotiating for greater contributions by the OECD countries is not a successful one. COP 28 after the G20 summit manifested this. To deal with climate adaptability and mitigation requires immense funding. Here India could try and use hybrid solutions where smaller funds are collected and leveraged through international markets to generate a larger fund for implementing sustainable projects. Hybrid finance with adequate guarantees and more participative involvement of the host country could be a way forward. This is still nascent, but there are ways to do this which are now under discussion.

A third area is the creation of a just energy transition simultaneously with LiFE to bring sustainability into lifestyles. This will improve human life and its quality and protect communities and countries from the growing challenges that they face.

As the SDGs acquire greater momentum in attracting direct investment at the grassroots level, impact investment is also the subject of India's trilateral cooperation efforts particularly in Africa, both in the private sector and through the Ministry of External Affairs (MEA). Funds are established where G7 countries such as the UK, France, Germany, and Japan, besides the EU, have taken slow steps towards contribution. The India-German Sustainability Development Cooperation is now working on such projects in Peru, Cameroon, Ghana and Malawi, while the UK and the MEA have established an impact fund for similar purposes. With France, a fund for the Indo-Pacific is underway.

A fourth important area is the digital economy. Dealing with digital public infrastructure, cyber security solutions for MSMEs, Sustainable Development Goals and the use of geospatial technologies are under discussion. India can utilise mechanisms for a digitally skilled future-ready workforce, which would help to implement the Industrial Revolution 4.0 and beyond. Therefore, digital public infrastructure, cyber security of the digital economy and digital skilling are essential priorities. These are best pursued through an expanded and diversified ITEC program.

A new working group on Disaster Risk Reduction was established under India's presidency to modulate the priorities through the G20 to undertake multi-disciplinary research and exchange best practices on disaster risk reduction. The creation of a 'Loss and Damage' fund at COP 27 in November 2022 for vulnerable countries hit hard by climate disasters is good intent without substance but COP 28 showed its limitations. The Indian initiative for prompt responses to Turkey and Syria beyond its neighbourhood, through its NDMA and NDRF, showed that example is more important than precept.

Self-Help Fund

Should the Global South not aim to help itself rather than cry hoarse over unfulfilled expectations from others? The Global South should have its own Self-Help Fund. The impact investment movement, where the Indian impact investing model is a good example, could be expanded. It attracts investors from the G7 and beyond. Its project implementation is effectively undertaken among developing countries. The main focus here is to have priorities directed by India and the main countries in the Global South like Indonesia, South Africa and Brazil who will contribute to, manage and direct the funds activity. Other G20 members and beyond would be welcome to contribute to their self-help groups for the SDGs but priority setting and project approval will be by the Global South countries

India has shown great empathy for Africa and the Global South and emphasised years of cooperation with Africa in the spirit of the 'Harambee Factor.' This has received considerable impetus through immense efforts under India's G20 presidency. India's presidency of the G20, with its open-hearted theme *Vasudhaiva Kutumbakam* could truly lead to One Earth, One Family, One Future. This was celebrated in a diverse and non-traditional manner through twelve months of India's G20 presidency, leaving a lasting legacy of the world acting in the spirit of one big family.

SECTION 3

BROADENING THE AGENDA

India's Legacy: Promoting Environmentally Responsible and Sustainable Development

VIBHA DHAWAN

In recent years, the global discourse on environmental sustainability and sustainable development has gained unprecedented momentum. As nations grapple with the pressing challenges posed by climate change, resource depletion, and ecological degradation, India has emerged as a prominent advocate for a comprehensive and inclusive approach to addressing these issues. The United Nations Intergovernmental Panel on Climate Change (IPCC) released in 2023 has unequivocal evidence that we are way off track in maintaining global warming to 1.5 degrees Celsius. This is also the year that India assumed the presidency of the G20, offering a unique opportunity to provide global leadership and shape the climate and social equity agenda from the perspective of the Global South. The theme for India's G20 Presidency, 'Vasudhaiva Kutumbakam' (One Earth, One Family, One Future), reflected India's outlook on fostering global cooperation and solidarity for a sustainable and inclusive future.

The theme underscores the need for global unity, collaboration, and collective efforts to build a resilient and equitable world that respects the principles of sustainable development as articulated in the Brundtland Commission Report as Our Common Future, "development that meets the needs of the present without compromising the ability of future generations to meet their own needs." India's G20 presidency places emphasis on human-centric development, green initiatives, cooperation in the fields of technology, inclusivity and holistic growth. Apart from emphasising collective action, our Hon'ble Prime Minister has eloquently articulated, "… a divided world cannot fight a common challenge. That is why our approach during our G20 presidency and otherwise has been to unify the world on this issue for what can be done. The poor and the planet, both need to be helped. India is moving ahead on this with not only a positive attitude but also a mindset of driving solutions" and in a way, this sets the agenda and indicates the next course of collective action.

India: Voice for the Global South

By championing equitable and fast-tracked actions, India has not only emerged as an architect of the global agenda but also a driver of change, sustainability and growth in the Global South.

As the impact of climate change is particularly pronounced in the Global South, India is amplifying the key challenges, opportunities and aspirations of developing and developed economies and calls for unified action. India's leadership in climate action has been to emphasise bringing together global opportunities and capacities in an equitable manner. India pioneered and showed leadership in setting up the International Solar Alliance (ISA), and has also collaborated with fellow G20 members to establish large-scale green hydrogen production capacity. India has pushed for transformative ideas.

India, positioned as an energy hub, could offer sustainable energy solutions at affordable rates, potentially resolving the overarching energy challenge. India has shown through the recent success of Chandrayaan that we can develop successful technologies just at a fraction of the cost of many technologically advanced countries. Underscoring the urgent need to scaling up finance for executing the collective vision of fostering global cooperation and solidarity for a sustainable and inclusive future, the Indian G20 presidency has set forth a blueprint to achieve the spirit of 'One Earth, One Family, One Future', which can fructify only with the inclusion of the Global South in the pursuit of a low-carbon climate-resilient world.

India's role as a voice for the Global South is integral to international discourse and decision-making. India's active engagement and leadership reflect the nation's commitment to promoting fairness, equity, and sustainable development on a global scale, while also advocating for the specific needs and priorities of developing countries.

Leading Energy Transition for a Just and Resilient Future

As the world's required capacity of energy increases with each passing day, the need for clean energy sources has never been higher. However, a balance between energy sustainability, affordability and reliability is imperative.

At the heart of India's sustainable development strategy is its commitment to climate action and the promotion of renewable energy sources. As part of its G20 presidency, India has championed the development and implementation of ambitious climate goals, and aligned with the objectives of the Paris Agreement. India's ambitious target of net zero emissions by 2070 and to obtain 50 per cent of its power generation capacity from renewable energy sources by 2030, showcases its determination to transition towards a low-carbon energy future.

Demonstrating remarkable progress, India has surpassed its commitment made during the 21st Conference of the Parties (COP 21) – Paris Summit by deriving 40 per cent of its power capacity from non-fossil fuel sources –achieving this milestone nearly a decade ahead of time. Notably, the proportion of solar and wind energy in India's energy portfolio has experienced a remarkable surge. Among major economies, India stands out for the unparalleled growth of its renewable energy sector, with projections indicating the doubling of new capacity additions by 2026. India also boasts a prominent standing as a significant producer of modern bioenergy and aims to significantly upscale its application across various sectors.

In this transformative journey, green hydrogen emerges as a pivotal player in achieving the net-zero aspiration. India's ambition to emerge as a global epicentre for green hydrogen production and exports is notable, with the potential to generate a considerable demand of five million tonnes –replacing conventional grey hydrogen in industries like refineries and fertilisers. This transformative shift could translate to the mitigation of 28 million tonnes of CO_2 emissions for this initial volume, with the potential for a monumental 400 million tonnes of CO2 abatement by 2050 as the green hydrogen economy evolves and flourishes. With regard to this, the Government of India proposed initiatives such as the proposed solar cities and parks, the National Green Hydrogen Mission, and the Green Energy Corridor. It is also rolling out policy measures and incentives that enable the uptake of green energy and technology, including the production-linked incentive (PLI) scheme for entities that set up manufacturing facilities for clean technology. As a large developing economy with over 1.3 billion people, India's climate adaptation and mitigation ambitions are not just transformational for India but for the entire planet.

A more concrete announcement under India's G20 presidency is the Global Biofuel Alliance led by Brazil, India and the USA. The alliance seeks to accelerate sustainable biofuels deployment in support of the global energy transition and aims to foster cooperation and enhance the adoption of sustainable biofuels, particularly within the transportation sector, including aviation and shipping. The shift becomes all the more important in the light of international regulations such as cross-border carbon tax.

Positive Agenda: Lifestyle for the Environment (LiFE)

The energy crisis looms large over the G20 countries especially as their development depends on ensuring energy security and with developmental progress energy usage is bound to increase. Once again, appealing to the concept of 'One Earth, One Planet, One Family' and also recognising the diversity of cultures, India's Mission Lifestyle for the Environment (LiFE) rallies the global community, both individuals and institutions, to embrace LiFE as a worldwide grassroots mass movement. We must realise that every individual is responsible for and is impacted by climate change, though to varying degrees.

The essence of LiFE revolves around a shift from wasteful consumption to purposeful and conscious utilisation, safeguarding and conserving our environment and simultaneously achieving the SDGs. LiFE places the onus on each individual and the collective to lead a lifestyle harmonious with the Earth, devoid of harm. India in its G2O presidency advances the concept of LiFE, and encourages individuals to live a sustainable lifestyle and safeguard resources for future generations. It emphasises individual accountability and reflection as to how each of us can conduct our daily life in a more sustainable way.

The Road Ahead

To sum up, India's approach to the environment and sustainable development during its G20 presidency reflects a forward-looking and comprehensive strategy that addresses the complex challenges of the 21st century. By prioritising climate action and renewable energy, India is setting a positive example for global cooperation and leadership in the pursuit of a more sustainable future. India has done this through its effective advocacy for the Global South, setting an example for sustainable energy transitions and pioneering the LiFE mission that promotes responsible climate behaviour. As India continues to lead discussions and initiatives within the G20 framework, its commitment to environmental preservation and sustainable development serves as a beacon of hope and inspiration for nations around the world. By showcasing the interconnectedness of economic growth, social well-being, and environmental protection, India's G20 presidency offers valuable insights into how a balanced and holistic approach can pave the way for a more resilient, inclusive and prosperous future for all.

REFERENCES

Global Biofuel Alliance. One of the priorities under India's G20 Presidency, PIB, Delhi, https://pib.gov.in/PressReleasePage.aspx?PRID=1898274

G20 DWG. India's Mission LiFE for Green Transition, PBNS, https://newsonair.com/2022/12/16/g20-dwg-indias-mission-life-for-green-transition/

'G20 transition to clean energy should include global South: PM', *Statesman* News Service. https://www.thestatesman.com/india/g20-transition-to-clean-energy-should-include-global-south-pm-1503203319.html

'India's clean energy transition is rapidly underway, benefiting the entire world – Analysis', International Environmental Agency, https://www.iea.org/commentaries/india-s-clean-energy-transition-is-rapidly-underway-benefiting-the-entire-world

21

Harnessing Trade and Investment for Inclusive Prosperity

MOHAN KUMAR

India took over the G20 presidency from Indonesia in what has turned out to be a seamless transition. The Bali G20 meeting of Trade and Investment Ministers emphasised the importance of policy coherence between trade, investment and industry to support the implementation of the United Nations 2030 Agenda and the achievement of the Sustainable Development Goals (SDGs). This will provide a basis for a strong foundation for a resilient, strong, sustainable and inclusive global economic recovery.

Taking off from the above, the Trade and Investment Ministers of the G20 countries met in Jaipur, India, on 24 and 25 August. The Ministers reached a groundbreaking consensus on concrete and action-oriented deliverables which have been adopted in the Outcome Document of Trade Ministerial Meeting held in Jaipur. Each of these outcomes is considered below briefly:

(1) Reform of the WTO was the centre of discussions among the ministers. They reaffirmed that a rule-based, non-discriminatory, fair, open, inclusive, sustainable and transparent multilateral trading system, with the WTO at its core, is indispensable to achieve inclusive growth and prosperity. The ministers also committed to reinforce cooperation on international trade and investment to achieve the SDGs. On the WTO, the Ministerial Conference (MC)

12 Outcome Document was reaffirmed on the need to pursue WTO reform through a member-driven, open, inclusive and transparent process that must address the interests of all its members, including on development issues. The ministers stressed that the development dimension should be an integral part of such deliberations. Interestingly, the importance of the ongoing negotiations in the WTO was underscored by the G20 Ministers.

Comment: The WTO can remain at the 'core' of the multilateral trading system only if it is reformed and made functional in all three aspects: negotiating aspect, dispute settlement aspect and trade monitoring aspect. As far as negotiations are concerned, a call has to be taken (including by countries like India) whether pluri-lateral negotiations can be housed in the WTO and how it can be taken forward. On dispute settlement, is it possible to revert to the two-tier dispute settlement mechanism which was the jewel in the crown of the WTO. If so, can this be done latest by 2024? Last, but not the least, on the trade monitoring function of the WTO, members like China have to be more forthcoming in terms of sharing information on their trade policy regime. India has done a great job by emphasising the 'development dimension' in the WTO deliberations which should help all countries of the Global South. Indeed, the WTO should align its work more and more towards enabling its members to achieve the SDGs. This is important because the latest Global Sustainable Development Report which will be released by the UN Secretary-General in September in New York makes sombre reading. It is said that half the world has been left behind in terms of achievement of SDGs by 2030. Against this background, the forthcoming WTO Ministerial Conference in Abu Dhabi in the last week of February 2024 is important. It really is a make-or-break moment for the WTO.

(2) Resilient Global Value Chains (GVCs) were discussed at length and the ministers vowed to continue their efforts to promote and uphold not just resilient but also inclusive GVCs. The ministers highlighted the importance of identifying digital solutions that

can help a high level of GVC participation and revive GVC growth. Enhanced regulatory cooperation, capacity building efforts and transparency in rules and regulations were emphasised.

Comment: Again, India spoke for the Global South when it talked of increasing participation in GVCs and reviving their growth. An impressive 'Generic Framework for mapping GVCs' was outlined as a concrete step in this regard including some guiding principles for collaboration. This should be of enormous help for countries of the Global South.

(3) MSMEs were given great importance so much so that there was a 'Jaipur Call for Action for enhancing MSMEs access to information'. The ministers recognised the critical role played by MSMEs, including women-owned or women-led MSMEs in world economies. It was recognised that limited or inadequate access to information, finance and markets are three key challenges faced by MSMEs. The main recommendation of the ministers was to scale up existing portals that provide business and trade-related information to MSMEs.

The International Trade Centre (ITC) was tasked to come up with a detailed implementation plan in consultation with UNCTAD and WTO regarding their Global Trade Helpdesk.

Comment: This is an excellent and practical step which will help MSMEs, especially those belonging to the Global South.

(4) Logistics for trade was an important matter for discussion. The ministers rightly believed that widespread adoption of paperless trade will drive productivity gains and economic growth by reducing trade costs and lowering barriers to entry for MSMEs. The ministers endorsed non-binding 'High-Level Principles on Digitisation of Trade Documents' and urged all countries to make efforts to implement them. Some of these principles are: Neutrality, Security, Trust, Interoperability, Data Privacy, Reliability and Voluntary sharing of Data.

Comment: The digital divide is real and came into sharp focus during the COVID pandemic. Countries of the Global South need to invest more not just in electronic infrastructure but also in their people to ensure digital literacy. Without this, they run the risk of being left behind.

(5) The Indian presidency has proposed a G20 Standards Dialogue in 2023 which will bring together members, policymakers, regulators, standard-setting bodies and other stakeholders to discuss topics of common interest such as good regulatory practices and standards. This will be held in partnership with World Standards Cooperation and seek to promote capacity building and exchange of best practices.

Comment: One of the biggest impediments to trade and investment that countries of the Global South face is the standards and regulations imposed by the developed countries on goods and services from the Global South. It is important that these are discussed between all stake holders with a view to removing unnecessary barriers to trade, harmonising minimum standards even while ensuring that the principles of necessity, non-discrimination and proportionality are scrupulously adhered to.

(6) The importance of services for the economies of the Global South cannot be overemphasised. In this regard, the initiative of India to come up with a 'Presidency Compendium of best practices for Professional Services' must be commended.

Comment: As exporters of professional services, countries like India have to face barriers in advanced countries and it is worthwhile to highlight best practices in this crucial area. At the end of the day, mutual recognition agreements are critical for professional services exports.

(7) It is hard to have a meeting these days without the war in Ukraine being discussed. The G20 Trade and Investment Ministers meeting in Jaipur were no different. In the event, this was the only paragraph which did not attract a consensus. What the G20 Trade and Investment Ministers did was to repeat verbatim the language from the G20 Bali Leaders Declaration. This paragraph on Ukraine found a consensus in Bali including from Russia and China present

there. But as has now become common, Russia has changed position since Bali and has been objecting to the Bali language. The Jaipur meeting was no exception. Russia stated that the one paragraph on Ukraine be considered as the 'Chair's Summary' and not the outcome document produced based on consensus. China gave diplomatic support to Russia on this.

Comment: With positions hardening since Bali, this is not a surprise. Indeed, barring a breakthrough, this may also provide a template for India when it comes up with a Leaders' Declaration following the New Delhi Summit on 9 and 10 September.

The Road Ahead

India held a hugely successful G20 Summit in Delhi in September 2023. The most remarkable thing was that well before the last day of the Summit, a consensus document was announced by Prime Minister Modi to universal relief and acclamation. The consensus language on the war in Ukraine took everyone by surprise. While the Bali language could be construed as taking sides, the Delhi Summit decided to put the war in Ukraine in its proper perspective. India as a host played a big part in acting as a bridge between the G7 on the one hand and Russia/China on the other hand. India also batted for the Global South and led a group of countries such as Indonesia, Brazil and South Africa to strike a compromise. For G20, this was an existential moment. If the Delhi G20 Summit had failed to produce a consensus, it may well have dented the credibility of G20 itself. This was in fact one of the main reasons why the G7 countries chose to compromise on the language on Ukraine despite taking a tough line before the Summit began. In my latest book '*India's Moment*' I have summarised the Delhi G20 Summit thus and I give excerpts below:

(1) India showcased itself in all its glory by making the G20 'people-centric'.

(2) India succeeded in being the voice of the Global South and in fact held the second Voice of the Global South summit after the G20 meeting. Facilitating the admission of the African Union as a member of the G20 was a masterstroke.

(3) India tried to be a rule-shaper rather than a rule-taker for the first time. This was evident in areas such as digital public infrastructure, Global Biofuel Alliance, Green Hydrogen Innovation Centre and Deccan High-Level Principles on Food Security and Nutrition.

(4) On the sidelines of the Summit, India launched initiatives such as the IMES (India-Middle East-Europe-Economic Corridor) by far the most ambitious global infrastructure project undertaken by India involving the USA, the EU, France, Germany, Italy, the UAE and Saudi Arabia.

(5) All this points to the fact that India's transition from a balancing power to a leading power is well under way.

India-US Partnership and India's G20 Success

MUKESH AGHI

It was a feather in the cap for India's deft diplomacy. India's presidency of the G20 epitomized diplomatic cooperation and a consensus towards building a more egalitarian world as the leaders of G20 nations and their respective delegations adopted a declaration that called for peace and prosperity in all parts of the world.

Prime Minister Narendra Modi echoed the thought that it was time to work towards ending a 'global trust deficit' and focus on bridging the gap between the developed economies and the Global South. This G20 Summit rightly identified lacunas in food and energy security and the need to address debt vulnerabilities in low and middle-income countries, as the global community works to strengthen and reform multilateral institutions.

In one of the coldest winters in 2024, we also witnessed some of the hottest summer months in 2023. This is a clarion call to tackle climate change and the need for effective climate financing as we transit to a green economy with renewables as the primary source of energy.

India's presidency offered a uniform voice for emerging economies and the Global South, as the African nations became permanent members of the G20.

Recognising women as the backbone of the economy, India's presidency highlighted the importance of 'Nari Shakti', and empowering women at the centre of economic progress.

With regard to economic progress, the landmark India-Middle East-European Corridor (IMEEC) is a commendable achievement in building new trade links and creating new shipping and transport planes that will boost digital connectivity and bring the I2U2 closer, openly, and transparently. There are some immediate challenges, as the war in Gaza and West Asia and troubled trade routes in the Red Sea could delay this trade link and create immediate short-term delays in global trade routes.

The joint statement by President Joe Biden and Prime Minister Narendra Modi on the sidelines of the historic summit is a further harbinger of the strength of the strategic partnership. Both Washington and New Delhi have reaffirmed their commitment to strengthening bilateral ties and reinforce the strong bonds between two of the world's leading democracies.

The statement builds on the momentum from the historic state visit in June and reflects the importance of the India-USA Major Defence Partnership, through expanded cooperation in new and emerging domains such as space and AI and accelerated defence industrial collaboration.

The efforts of the USA and India towards clean energy diversification, linking defence industrial ecosystems, secure and trusted telecommunications, resilient supply chains, cooperation in the fields of biotechnology, and global digital inclusion will help emerging economies prosper as we seek to safeguard a free and open Indo-Pacific.

Looking Back

Prime Minister Narendra Modi had articulated India's vision in that the G20 Summit would espouse the importance of equitable growth and a shared future for all. The theme said it all, 'Vasudhaiva Kutumbakam', or 'One Earth, One Family, One Future'. Prime Minister Modi emphasised that India's presidency came at a time of global economic and geopolitical headwinds and that the summit will voice the concerns of the Global South.

Weeks before the summit, in Johannesburg, South Africa, at the BRICS Summit, Prime Minister Modi had proposed that the African Union become a permanent member of the G20.

Advantage and Challenge

India's place on the global stage is now established. As the world's most populous country with one of the fastest-growing economies, India serves as a key bridge between the emerging economies and the Group of 7 (G7) bloc. India, apart from advocating a more egalitarian representation for the Global South, is also looked upon as a key arbiter in the tensions between Russia and the West with the ongoing conflict in Ukraine.

With the G20 presidency, India had the herculean task of bridging the trust deficit that lies between Moscow and the West, as tensions in Europe exacerbated the economic crisis of food and energy price volatility. Previous G20 meetings since December 2022, when India took over the presidency from Indonesia, failed to realise a joint communiqué between the member-nations as the deadlock ensued. Unfortunately, consensus and a solution continue to elude.

The G20 meetings previously had deliberated on rising debt, sustainable development, climate action, and food security, among other issues that affect low- to middle-income countries.

While President Putin skipped the summit and deputized his Foreign Minister Sergey Lavrov to be Moscow's voice and articulate their concerns, President Biden visited New Delhi for the first time as the 46th President. President Biden addressed a broad range of economic issues, including the ongoing conflict between Russia and Ukraine.

Bilateral Ties in Multilateral Fora

The world's largest and oldest democracies will go to the polls in 2024.uch is made about the outcome of the elections and what it would mean for New Delhi and Washington. The year 2023 evinced that the synergy between Washington and New Delhi is stronger than ever as trade hit near $ 200 billion, with the USA now India's largest trading partner.

President Biden and Prime Minister Modi met once again after a historic state visit by Prime Minister Modi to the USA in June, which reaffirmed the strength of the strategic partnership and elevated it to new heights. Washington and New Delhi inked crucial deals in critical and emerging technology, with the jet engines deal and quantum computing to semiconductor investments, and from drone technology and artificial intelligence to underwater cables. With ISRO's recent success, there will be many more opportunities for collaboration in space between NASA and ISRO.

The threat of climate change means a conscientious shift from fossil fuels to a clean energy economy as both New Delhi and Washington reaffirm their commitment to this sector. The people-to-people ties remain the bedrock of this relationship as education and cultural links are further cemented.

Economic Vision

The core mandate of the G20 nations remained to promote economic growth and development. Prime Minister Modi made it clear that these goals cannot be achieved without addressing the concerns and achieving a consensus in the Global South.

A slew of problems from tackling climate change to reforming multilateral development banks and multilateral institutions such as the World Bank and International Monetary Fund required a consensus-building approach. The focus on development banks remains critical as infrastructure investments and development remain a key priority, especially as the security situation worsens in the sub-Saharan region.

The geopolitics of the South China Sea and territorial disputes have brought Tokyo, Canberra, Washington, and New Delhi together in the Indo-Pacific QUAD, but the G20 will bring to the fore the priority for maritime security and economic fishing lanes. The priority in the Indo-Pacific remains twofold: economic growth and investments in emerging economies and adhering to and upholding a rule-based international order.

Prime Minister Modi made India's digital transformation a key priority for the G20 Summit, addressing the debt stress plaguing emerging economies, and collectively finding solutions to climate goals, which shows that no part of the world is insulated from this threat.

Elevating Manufacturing

As India sets its sights on becoming a 5-trillion-dollar economy and is expected to grow from the fifth largest to the third largest economy, the imperative remains to generate 12-15 million jobs annually to accommodate the influx of new entrants into the workforce.

While India's information technology prowess is well established, the burden cannot be shouldered solely by the services sector. There is a concerted effort to grow India's manufacturing economy, especially in high-tech manufacturing. This sector is scalable and will provide mass employment for semi-skilled labourers, foster essential economic mobility, and contribute to the GDP of individual, thereby underscoring the economic competitiveness among different states within the federal structure.

Semiconductors: The New Oil

The focus is on semiconductors in the critical and emerging technology domain as AI dominance enters the geopolitical fray. Companies need to look at a 'China-plus-one' model in a dual effort to rebuild supply chains and avoid bottlenecks and supply chain vulnerability after the COVID-19 pandemic of 2020. This has accentuated the necessity to diversify manufacturing locations and explore alternative markets for advanced products.

India stands out in this regard. To bridge the deficit with Beijing, the government in New Delhi is focused on initiatives like 'Make in India' and 'Production Linked Incentives'. The policy outcomes from the state visit in June 2023 show that manufacturing is vital to both American and Indian economies, and both New Delhi and Washington continue to share geopolitical and economic alignment in an era of cooperative manufacturing.

Apple CEO Tim Cook's India's visit to inaugurate Apple's maiden retail store in the country holds profound significance and reinforces the tech giant's confidence in India's ecosystem and extends an invitation to fellow Fortune 250 enterprises to participate in the 'Make in India' initiative. It is also a belief in India's supply chain capabilities, and adds confidence as a prime destination for American manufacturers, particularly within the expansive consumer electronics domain that aligns with India's huge consumer market.

A newly privatised Air India meant augmented purchasing power to procure additional aircraft from both Boeing and Airbus.

The agreement with Boeing not only bolstered commercial ties between the USA and India but was also hailed as a 'historic agreement' by President Biden and Prime Minister Modi. This accord resonated as a pivotal catalyst for the American manufacturing sector, a critical point of discussion as America heads to the polls in 2024.

From the sea to the stars, in securing a free and open Indo-Pacific to the success of its space mission, to energising a clean energy economy with the electrification of vehicles and the ubiquity of digital payments and the growth of the digital economy, the G20 Summit and India's presidency is a harbinger of growth for the Indian economy.

23

Global Partnership for Sustainable Development: The New Delhi Summit and Beyond

NAGESH KUMAR

Established initially as a forum of the largest economies for coordinated action to address the challenges thrown by global financial crises, the G20 has evolved over the years into the premier forum for advancing international economic cooperation. India's G20 presidency in 2023 ushered in an important new phase in its evolution where, for the first time, all the Troika members were from the Global South. The countries of the Global South continue to helm the influential forum for the next two years with Brazil'spresidency in 2024 followed by South Africa in 2025.

Since the adoption of the G20 Action Plan on the 2030 Agenda for Sustainable Development in 2016, sustainable development has enjoyed an important place in the discussions at G20 summits. The India's presidency has placed sustainable development at the centre of the international cooperation agenda by focusing attention on the issues of concern to the Global South (including through convening the Voices of the Global South Summit hosted in preparation for and after the G20 New Delhi Summit), besides enhancing its inclusivity by bringing in the African Union as a full member.

The major thrust of the India's presidency was to strengthen the means of implementation for accelerating progress towards the achievement of Sustainable Development Goals (SDGs). Various assessments have confirmed that most developing countries are not only on track to achieve the SDGs at the mid-point of the 2030 deadline, but progress has been reversed in several targets. The poly-crises comprising the COVID-19 pandemic, the food and energy security challenges resulting from conflicts such as the wars raging in Ukraine and the Middle East, and the debt crisis, are threatening to push 175 million people back into extreme poverty.

The primacy of the sustainable development agenda and its means of implementation as the key priorities for India's presidency is evident in the New Delhi Declaration[1] and in the 2023 G20 New Delhi Update compiled by the Development Working Group (DWG) to summarise the key issues, agreements and decisions adopted by different sectoral bodies and groups of the G20 under the India's presidency.[2]

Among the most critical means of implementation for the SDGs and climate action goals are access to finance and technology. This article focuses on these two critical areas and reviews the progress made under G20 India's presidency and its prospects under Brazil's presidency.

Advancing Sustainable Development Agenda

The key prerequisite for the achievement of SDGs remains having a strong, sustainable, balanced and inclusive growth, which also formed the focus of the opening section of the New Delhi Declaration. It continued with a full section devoted to Accelerating Actions on SDGs which re-committed the members to SDGs besides concrete actions focused on hunger and malnutrition, food and energy security, health, quality education, and the SDG targets that matter for developing countries.

The successful implementation of the SDGs in developing countries requires global cooperation and partnership. The 2030 Agenda adopted at the United Nations Summit in 2015, therefore, included a reinvigorated global partnership covering finance, technology, trade (market access), capacity-building, and data, monitoring and accountability. The New Delhi Declaration has also addressed some of these issues including through sectoral ministerial and working group meetings. One of the key outcomes was the Green Development Pact for a Sustainable Future covering important issues of macroeconomic risks stemming from climate change and addressing them through mainstreaming lifestyles for the environment or sustainable development (LiFE). It is an important concept coming from India, designing a circular economy, implementing just and inclusive energy transitions; delivering on climate and sustainable finance including for future cities, conserving and restoring ecosystems, harnessing the ocean-based economy, ending plastic pollution, and building resilient infrastructure.

Financing Sustainable Development

Given that finance is the key constraint faced by developing countries in implementing their climate action goals and achieving SDGs, delivering on climate and sustainable finance received considerable attention in the G20 process. The Declaration recognised the need for staggering magnitudes of resources – USD 5.9 trillion before 2030 by developing countries for implementing their NDCs, besides USD 4 trillion annually for clean energy technologies by 2030 to achieve net zero by 2050 – and called on multilateral development banks (MDBs) and funds to strengthen their efforts.

As reformed MDBs could play an important role in climate finance, they were a critical issue, especially for developing countries Therefore, a separate section was devoted to Multilateral Institutions for the 21st Century, covering a review of the Capital Adequacy Framework, which could yield additional lending headroom of approximately USD 200 billion. An important initiative of India's G20 presidency was the appointment of the G20 Independent Expert Group (IEG) on Strengthening MDBs co-chaired by Mr. N. K. Singh of India and Prof. Larry Summers of the USA. The Singh-Summers panel has issued two reports, the first one was available before the New Delhi Summit.

The context for the IEG discussion was the fact that the global community has found it challenging to keep its development finance commitments, whether it is the 0.7 per cent of gross national income (GNI) as overseas development assistance (ODA) commitment made way back in the 1970s or $100 billion per annum in climate finance by 2020 made at COP15 in Copenhagen in 2009, but this was not achieved till 2023. SDGs and climate action cannot be undertaken with private finance because of their exorbitant cost. Given that multilateral development banks (MDBs) provide financing at the lowest cost to developing countries, an important solution that was discussed was enhancing the lending capacity of MDBs through reforms and their recapitalisation. Over the next five years, the MDB capital needs to at least treble, if not more. It is possible to enhance this with relatively modest resources. The fourth and final meeting of the G20 finance ministers and central bank governors (FMCBGs) held under India's presidency on 12-13 October 2023 in Marrakesh, Morocco, on the sidelines of the IMF/WB annual meetings, (post-New Delhi Summit) welcomed the IEG Report on Strengthening MDBs. FMCBGs have noted the need for transformative changes required in the vision of MDBs, operating models and financing capacities. The three building blocks that the FMCBGs have urged for consideration are private capital mobilisation, strengthening their financial capacity including through implementation of capital adequacy framework recommendations and capital increase, and urging MDBs to work together as a system. Going forward, they have called for continued work on the recommendations of the report for building better, bigger and more effective MDBs.[3] FMCBGs also agreed to collectively mobilise more headroom and concessional finance to boost the World Bank's capacity to support low and middle-income countries and hoped for an ambitious 21st Replennishment of the International Development Association (IDA21) to increase IDA financing capacity.

India's presidency has, therefore, managed to advance the critical finance agenda. One would expect that the proposals made by IEG and Finance Ministers would be followed up and implemented in earnest and lead to enhanced magnitudes of affordable finance to the countries of the Global South in the coming years for climate action and SDG implementation.

The development finance agenda, generated under India's presidency, would continue to remain an important one for the Brazil's presidency to take the momentum forward. Among other issues that would merit attention in the coming years including the reform of the governance structures of MDBs. Capital increases will have to go hand in hand with voice and representation reform, including the ability to appoint the heads of the Bretton Woods institutions. MDBs should also be made to help in building the absorptive capacity of developing member countries by the development of transformative projects in clean energy, sustainable transportation systems, sanitation, and sustainable forestry, among other areas, which were raised during a brainstorming session on the subject organised by the Institute for Studies in Industrial Development (ISID) and Boston University Development Policy Centre (BU/GDPC) in New Delhi in March 2023.[4]

Furthermore, innovative sources such as SDRs and carbon taxes need to complement the MDB reform. Regular issuance of special drawing rights (SDRs) and their utilisation is one such option. Carbon taxation is another innovative mechanism and has tremendous potential, especially in the North and some of the revenue can be used for international transfers. An International Financial Transactions Tax (IFTT) is another such possible innovative option to generate perpetual resources for climate action in the Global South. New calculations made by ISID-BUGDPC suggest that even a modest tax of 0.05 per cent could generate revenues of US$ 650 billion p.a., roughly equivalent to three-and-a-half times the annual flows of ODA,[5] hurting no one but speculators. Besides resources for climate action, IFTT could also provide another global public good by helping curb the volatility and disruptive consequences of short-term capital flows. IFTT was put on the G20 agenda at the 2009 Pittsburgh Summit in the aftermath of the global financial crisis. The 2011 Cannes Summit, however, failed to endorse the IFTT proposal, despite strong support from President Nicolas Sarkozy of France, and other European leaders. The changed context since 2011 warrants bringing IFTT back on the agenda. While the need for climate finance becomes more urgent by the day, limited fiscal space in developed countries dampens the prospects of plugging shortages of finance. The combined effects of the COVID-19 pandemic, the inflationary spiral stoked by the Ukraine war, food and energy security challenges, and the debt crisis, have stretched the budgets in both developed and developing countries. Over the past decade, the world has also suffered highly disruptive consequences of boom-bust cycles following monetary policy changes in developed countries – from the 'fragile five' of 2013-14 to the ongoing volatility in financial markets.[6] The IFTT has the unique ability to curb volatility while generating resources required for climate action. Given that it has been on the agenda in the past and a lot of analysis and discussion has already taken place, IFTT seems like a proverbial 'low-hanging fruit' waiting to be plucked. Hence, given its relevance in the changed context, it should be revived on the G20 agenda and taken forward.

Access to Technology and Sustainable Industrialisation

India's G20 presidency was able to focus on the equally important issue of technology access for sustainable development. The Leaders' Declaration recognised that technology can enable rapid transformations for bridging the existing digital divides and accelerating progress for inclusive and sustainable development. In that context, digital public infrastructure (DPI)'s emergence as an evolving concept can foster development in an inclusive manner. India offered to build a Global Digital Public Infrastructure Repository (GDPIR), as a virtual repository of DPI, voluntarily shared by G20 members and beyond. India also proposed the One Future Alliance as a voluntary initiative aimed at capacity building, and provide technical assistance and funding for implementing DPI in low and middle-income countries. The G20 Declaration also focused on safety, security, resilience and trust in the digital economy, policy and regulation of crypto assets, central bank digital currency, fostering digital ecosystems and harnessing of artificial intelligence (AI) responsibly for the benefit of all.

Therefore, the Indian presidency was able to advance the technology agenda especially in the emerging field of digital technology, which is increasingly becoming a defining aspect of the global economy. Brazil's G20 presidency will have to take the agenda forward from where the Indian presidency has left, and build upon it. There are also issues for discussion on affordable access to climate technologies which are so critical for a clean transition. The multilateral trade rules should facilitate the transfer of environmentally sound technologies. The agricultural Green Revolution in developing countries, for instance, was facilitated by the fact that the new technologies were available in the public domain. The vast majority of climate technologies, however, are developed in advanced countries and are covered by patents. Climate change, like the public health crisis, is a global emergency. In order to speed up climate action, the Trade Related Intellectual Property Rights (TRIPS) Agreement under WTO should be amended to extend flexibilities like compulsory licensing provisions for climate technologies, similar to the case of public health for developing countries. Similarly, to achieve the objective of Net Zero, the renewable energy capacity needs to expand in an unprecedented manner. However, the entire global value chain for renewable energy equipment is highly concentrated in a few countries. The productive capacity for renewable energy equipment needs to be enhanced massively in a diversified manner to foster their rapid deployment for clean transition, including through the use of industrial policy instruments such as domestic content requirements (DCRs). This would require multilateral trade rules like Trade-Related Investment Measures (TRIMs) under the World Trade Organisation to provide flexibilities for climate action. The G20 is the relevant forum for building consensus on these critical issues for climate action and sustainable development before they are taken to multilateral trade negotiations.7

To sum up, India's G20 presidency of G20 has managed to put reinvigorated global partnership at the centre stage of the agenda of the influential forum to fix the constraints of finance and technology for sustainable development and green transformation. Among many pioneering proposals brought forward, an important legacy of the India's presidency of G20 is the forward movement on the important issue of finance for sustainable development through a reform of MDBs. The India's presidency has also advanced the agenda of harnessing digital technology for inclusive and sustainable development and has offered to share its own development experiences with other developing countries.

Hopefully, the presidencies of Brazil and South Africa will continue to build on the momentum generated in New Delhi and put the challenges faced by the countries of the Global South at the centre of the G20 agenda in a true spirit of multilateralism and international development cooperation for building a more inclusive, sustainable, and resilient future for all!

NOTES

1. G20 India 2023, *G20 New Delhi Leaders' Declaration*, New Delhi, 9-10 September 2023.
2. https://www.g20.in/content/dam/gtwenty/gtwenty_new/document/G20-2023-New-Delhi-Update.pdf

3. https://www.g20.in/content/dam/gtwenty/gtwenty_new/document/Final_G20_
FMCBG_October_2023_Communique.pdf https://www.g20.in/content/dam/gtwenty/
gtwenty_new/document/Final_G20_FMCBG_October_2023_Communique.pdf
4. See ISID (2023) Finance and Global Economic Governance for Green Transformation:
Key Recommendations of ISID-BUGDPC Special T20 Roundtable, March 2023, https:/
/isid.org.in/wp-content/uploads/2023/05/PB2302.pdf.
5. Nagesh Kumar and Kevin Gallagher. 'Towards an Innovative Financing Mechanism for
Sustainable Development: Reviving International Financial Tax (IFTT) on the G20
Agenda,' *T20 Policy Brief,* June 2023.
6. Nagesh Kumar and Kevin Gallagher. 'G20 Also Needs to Act to Curb the Short-Term
Capital Flows and Fund Development,' *The Jakarta Post,* 29 October 2021, https://
www.thejakartapost.com/paper/2021/10/27/g20-needs-to-act-to-curb-short-term-capital-
flows-and-fund-development.html
7. See for more details, *ISID* (2023) op.cit. (Finance and Global Economic Governance for
Green Transformation: Key Recommendations of ISID-BUGDPC Special T20 Roundtable,
March 2023, https://isid.org.in/wp-content/uploads/2023/05/PB2302.pdf)

India's G20 Imprint:
Deepening Civil Society Connect

During the past year of India's presidency of the G20, the civil society engagement group or C20 saw an unprecedented degree of '*Jan Bhagidaari*' or people's participation in the country. In addition to the world-renowned Mata Amritanandamayi Devi or *Amma*, founder of the Mata Amritanandamayi Math who was nominated as chairperson, of the C20 core committee included Sri M of the Satsang Foundation, an eminent social reformer and educationist; Ms Nivedita Bhide of the Vivekananda Kendra, Kanya Kumari, and Swami Amritaswaroopananda, Puri, President of the Amrita Vishwa Vidyapeetham, India. Dr. Vinay Sahasrabuddhe, president of the Indian Council for Cultural Relations (ICCR) and vice-chairman of the Rambhau Mhalgi Prabodhini (RMP) was the patron of the C20 secretariat. Working along with this core committee, were the C20 steering committee and its international advisory committee that led the C20 activities with distinction and competence. Apart from the inaugural meeting on 16 January 2023, the C20 held its inception conference in Nagpur from 20 to 22 March 2023 and the C20 summit in Jaipur from 29 to 31 July 2023.

Over a short span of six months and under the guidance of its Chair, Sri Mata Amritanandamayi Devi (*Amma*), the C20 reached out to more than 4.5 million people. More than 12,040 events were held within the country as well as in foreign locations, including policy discussions, *chaupals* or consultation meetings with grassroots local CSOs, samaj-shalas or collective activities with partner organisations such as cleanliness drives or civic debates, ambassador programmes or youth activities in local schools and college campuses, and additional events such as inaugural events, webinars or side events. They also included mass outreach events organised in almost every state of India under the C20 aegis as well as at the international level in Australia, Canada, France, Germany, Greece, Israel, Kenya, Korea, Portugal, Spain, Switzerland and the USA. In all, they comprised participation by over 6,000 civil society organisations and other institutions, with participants from 154 countries.

Sixteen working groups were set up under C20 auspices at the start of the year in January 2023 covering both traditional themes of concern as well as entirely new themes proposed by the host country, India. The policy pack prepared for the summit in July 2023 covered some 240 pages and if the range of policy papers, White Papers and other documentation were to be included, the material produced under the Indian chair can be described as substantial. As a unique initiative, the C20 also conducted a worldwide grassroots survey with the help of 427 social workers and received 8,200-plus responses from 64 countries.

The G20 motto, '*Vasudhaiva Kutumbakam*', or 'One Earth, One Family One Future' was underlined in almost every aspect of their activity and remained the abiding leitmotif of the preoccupations of the various groups and subgroups during the year. While there was widespread recognition that at no time ever before has the world been as connected, interdependent and yet exposed to mutual vulnerabilities as it is today, the call by civil society around the world for increased cooperation between developed and developing nations, as well as among the countries of the Global South has often remained more a shibboleth than a reality. The pandemic pushed 200 million people below the poverty line, 100 million people have lost their jobs around the world and 75 countries are facing major debt crises. The global financial and debt crisis has affected nations across the world and it was thus incumbent upon the C20 to speak out. Sustained recovery from the multi-dimensional crisis facing the world today would require fundamental changes to the roles and functions that financial capital and the global financial architecture perform in the lives of humans and other living beings on this planet. The C20 gave a strong call to G20 governments to create and support better and new mechanisms that can help in fair and effective sovereign debt restructuring. In addition, it underlined that the G20 must develop ways to support the expansion of fiscal space to allow countries to maintain social protections and invest in resources that may limit the multiple overlapping emergencies such as climate change, public health inadequacies and growing inequality. The standing committee of the C20 on financial issues, in its policy brief, highlighted successive calls by developing countries for the democratisation of global tax governance under the auspices of the United Nations instead of the Organization for Economic Cooperation and Development (OECD), so that the voices of all affected states could be incorporated when formulating international decisions. International tax cooperation must be under a coherent institutional and normative framework. At the domestic level, the excessive concentration of wealth in the hands of a few individuals or households can lead to negative consequences for social and economic well-being. A wealth tax is needed to ensure the principle of equity and/or distributive justice and the G20 nations can take the lead in implementing this.

The committee also demanded that G20 governments call on multilateral development banks (MDBs) to update their mission, incentives, and operational approaches in order to better address global challenges, reduce poverty and achieve SDGs and for G20 national governments to focus on all the SDGs through their national strategies, without cherrypicking some SDGs over others. There was a strong feeling that civil society organisations must be co-opted as serious economic actors with non-trivial decision-making powers across all stages of implementation of the SDG agenda by MDBs and national governments. G20 nations must also focus on the crux of the issue with the private sector, which is to have industries pay for negative externalities that bring serious harm to the world's people as well as affect planetary health. Through the above mechanisms, the C20 called for a dramatic shift away from an economic growth model that used people and the planet as extractable resources, to one where the world's policymakers would work to reprogramme our economies to work for its people and the planet.

Main Recommendations of the C20 Working Groups

It may be apposite to recapitulate the recommendations of the other major working groups of the C20 as follows:

I. Sustainable and Resilient Communities

This working group did major work on a range of environmental issues: Enhancing regional climate resilience and disaster management capabilities by ensuring rights, access, and sustainability for food security, climate resilient agriculture by promoting sustainable practices and knowledge transfer; prioritising ecosystem restoration, biodiversity protection, sustainable water governance, and coastal conservation; climate-sensitive planning for climate-induced displacement; climate finance for inclusive and effective climate action; focusing on lifestyle changes and demand reduction, circular economy, deep decarbonisation; and fostering peace, harmony and compassion by integrating cultural values as well as rediscovering local traditions. Not enough funding has gone into adaptation. Multilateral institutions must be incentivised to do direct lending. New imaginative sources must be located in both private and public sectors. New structures are needed for credit enhancements, first-loss guarantees and better de-risking modalities. The resources needed are not in billions but in trillions of US dollars.

II. Integrated Holistic Health

The goal of this working group has been to promote a state of '*Samyukta Arogya*' – '*Samyukt*': Integrated, Holistic Health: Mind, Body and Environment. Aligned with the WHO definition of health, 'a state of complete physical, mental, and social well-being and not merely the absence of disease and infirmity', the C20 integrated holistic health working group (IHH-WG) 2023 iterates that health promotion and disease prevention must be addressed at the levels of mind, body, and environment. Building on commitments made by previous G20 leaderships, IHH-WG expands the scope of the United Nations Sustainable Development Goal 3 (UNSDG3), Good Health and Well-Being, proposing inclusive, equitable and holistic solutions for building healthy communities. The group's key policy recommendations align with G20 priorities: Universal health coverage; reduction in the cost of healthcare through preventive strategies; management of mental disorders and promotion of mental well-being; creating and implementing policies on One-Health, with an emphasis on antimicrobial resistance as well as advance efforts to tackle communicable and non-communicable diseases. Also, they sought to promote digital health strategies to reduce healthcare costs.

III. Technology Security and Transparency

The Technology, Security, and Transparency group made the following recommendations under four distinct verticals:

- **Technology for Empowerment:** This theme advocated enhancing accessibility and inclusivity by setting up infrastructure bridging the digital divide, promoting user-centric design in technology, establishing open-data policies, democratising e-commerce platforms, and investing in robust technological solutions to achieve the SDGs and creating an inclusive and fair digital society.
- **Security, Safety, and Resilience:** This theme underscored the importance of international cooperation and collaboration in cyber security, protection against cyber-attacks on critical infrastructure, establishing legal frameworks to counter online violence, especially towards vulnerable populations, and developing norms to prevent misuse of AI systems and regulating technologies that innately induce addictive tendencies and negatively affect the user's health and well-being.
- **AI and Data for Society:** This theme emphasises that ethical, fair, and safe deployment of technology must be ensured, the generation of high-quality datasets for marginalised communities is incentivised, and international regulations assigning liability for harm arising from technology are created.
- **Transparency, Trust, and Disinformation:** This theme proposed measures to combat disinformation, including developing a shared terminology and a comprehensive strategy, establishing national information networks, establishing an effective legal infrastructure, and enhancing transparency and trust within the technology supply chain.

A new 'GLIDES' initiative was also launched which will create a global alliance of CSOs working collectively to enable an inclusive, open, non-discriminatory, and fair digital society.

IV. Education and Digital Transformation

While technological advancements in education have the potential for socioeconomic benefits, digital transformation currently lacks inclusiveness and accessibility, exacerbating the digital divide and inequalities, and putting at risk critical and ethical behaviour as well as child protection. Collective efforts were needed to make education and training fit for purpose by adapting the current systems towards emerging social needs. These must involve:

(a) Promoting holistic education for development;

(b) Enabling early identification and swift intervention for persons with disabilities and learning difficulties;

(c) Ensuring equitable access and learning equity/opportunity audit;

(d) Promoting capacity building for emergency preparedness and safety;

(e) Adopting digital solutions along with low-tech solutions for remote areas, community engagement, and training, and promoting lifelong learning opportunities, stakeholder coordination, and international collaboration; and

(f) Promoting inclusive digital accessibility.

V. Gender Equality and Women's Empowerment

This group underlined the focus on women, transgender people, and other marginalised populations at the 'base of the pyramid', those who have the least access, opportunities, resources, and privileges. Cross-cutting recommendations included:

• Improving gender-disaggregated data collection to inform decision making;

• Integrating monitoring and evaluation into policy development for transparency and accountability;

• Allocating sufficient resources to gender equality policies and programmes; and

- Prioritising safety and security for girls and women.

The thematic recommendations focused on:

- Prioritising mental health and investing in accessible mental health services for women and girls by developing comprehensive national mental health education policies and integrating such policies into schools and workplaces.
- Expanding access to education, particularly for rural and marginalised women by addressing barriers such as safety concerns, inadequate sanitation facilities, and lack of digital infrastructure.
- Establishing gender-responsive learning centres, ensuring access for marginalised groups, improving existing infrastructure, and expanding internet connectivity are key goals.
- Engaging men and boys who are vital for achieving gender equality. Harmful social norms contribute to issues like violence against women; gender sensitisation and transformative education should be provided to various stakeholders.
- Ensuring disaster preparedness and management includes women and girls who are disproportionately affected.
- Mandating their representation in decision-making bodies, conducting gender and vulnerability assessments, providing gender-responsive training and collaborating with local organisations is essential.
- Promoting women's economic empowerment and enhancing financial inclusion and equal financing opportunities (25per cent in green and blue economies and priority procurement for women entrepreneurs) through collaboration between relevant institutions and organisations.

VI. Disability, Equity, and Justice

The policy suggestions covered a gamut of issues from education and employment to health, social protection and environment-related needs.

- *Education:* A greater understanding is required of the needs of children across disabilities, material in the local language, understanding the needs of diverse learning styles and requirements and addressing barriers to inclusion not limited to inaccessible transport and physical infrastructure. Their need for equitable access to digital infrastructure as well as support services communication aids and other facilities are also underscored.

- *Employment:* SDG Target 4.5 requires enabling policies and strategies to support access to technical and vocational education and training (TVET) programmes for persons with disabilities consistent with ILO standards, also with ILO Violence and Harassment Convention norms (No. 190) and (No. 206), and to address discrimination, harassment, and violence against persons with disabilities in the workplace.
- *Health:* The WG called for acknowledgement and design of disability inclusion as a necessary component of public health initiatives. A strong health policy and research agenda on disability inclusion should be implemented to develop interventions, address the vast inequities in healthcare access for persons with disabilities, and ensure that healthcare providers are well-trained and WASH programmes are accessible.
- *Social Protection:* An adaptive universal framework for social protection of persons with disabilities should be implemented.

VII. Lifestyle for Environment

The LiFE tried to include values, concepts, instruments and actionable proposals for individuals and communities through a holistic Indian perspective of global well-being or '*Sumangalam*'. These included decentralisation, harmony, respecting diversity, a sense of responsibility, and promoting local. They stressed a range of technology interventions from food to fashion to reduce loss and waste and promote eco-efficient supply chains.

VIII. SDG16+ and Enhancing Civic Space

The SDG 16-plus WG stressed that the financing gap to fund the SDGs agenda is huge, around $4.2 trillion per year for the least developed countries. Meanwhile, more and more countries are facing major fiscal imbalances due to rising public debt, increasing healthcare and pension costs, and other long-term liabilities.

If SDG 16 is the key to addressing peace and security within communities, and partnerships between states, the private sector and civil society as underlined in SDG 17 were equally critical to realise the SDGs. This is true, especially with respect to the alliances for digital public infrastructure, coalitions for environmental sustainability, and public-private partnerships for disaster response. In respect of the need to provide better public goods for the global community, the rapid scaling up in India of public digital platforms like *Aadhaar*, unified payment interface (UPI), digital signature, DigiLocker along with the adoption of AI in fintech and high-speed internet services have contributed tremendously to providing swift, secure, paperless and cashless service delivery and can be a model for emulation elsewhere.

IX. Diversity, Inclusion and Mutual Respect

The WG underlined the urgency of inclusion of those left behind in the development process due to want, disability, disease or neglect. This comprised inclusion policies for LGBTQAI, indigenous communities and support for traditional practices. The WG's recommendations focused on avoiding fixed binaries, preserving cultural diversity, building knowledge bases and incorporating traditional knowledge into policy-making and education systems.

X. 'Sewa', Philanthropy and Volunteerism

The Indian concept of 'Sewa' embodies voluntarism based on selflessness and the desire to create a positive change in the world on the basis of the fundamental value of giving back to society, fostering empathy, and making a positive impact on the lives of others. The WG called for:

(a) The creation of a global alliance of individuals and civil society organisations to facilitate Sewa on a global scale.

(b) Utilising the experiences and talents of the elderly and retirees for nation-building purposes and mentoring of youth.

(c) Establishing a global network of civil societies and voluntary organisations practising Sewa in different countries, and

(d) Developing a compendium of exemplary Sewa practices from G20
countries to foster cross-country learning, inspire new initiatives,
and promote collaboration among nations.

XI. Delivering Democracy

This WG's report called for basing democracy on native models of
governance, native values and ethos, and best practices and learning. It
called for the engagement of young people in democratic processes and to
inculcate respect for democratic processes and institutions at school and
university levels.

It also emphasised practising grassroots democracy at the village level
by respecting the individual as the cornerstone of the democratic process.
It spoke of adapting digital democracy by expanding digital and internet
footprints countrywide and using social media intelligently. It also spoke
of responsible citizenry, responsive governance, and direct or indirect
participation by the people in governance as well as in the assertion of
their rights of self-governance.

XII. River Revival and Water Management

This working group proposes several recommendations for river revival
and water management that emphasise the importance of maintaining the
natural flow and self-purification capacity of rivers, as well as protecting
water resources as commons. They call for government stewardship,
including respecting citizens' rights and relationships with water, preventing
environmentally costly projects, and implementing pollution prevention
laws. The involvement of diverse stakeholders, such as indigenous
communities, NGOs, and experts, is also highlighted. The G20 is urged
to leverage technology, strengthen cross-border cooperation, and consider
environmental factors in valuing water resources. The approach should be
integrated, scalable, participatory, and supported by sustainable financing.

Best Practices (*Udaaharans*)

As a unique initiative and apart from policy recommendations, during
2023, the C20 also gathered and highlighted a series of 'best practices' or

Udaaharans from hundreds of civil society organisations that gave substance to the development aspirations of the common people in their daily lives.

To recall some important initiatives that were deeply inspiring and which were showcased in the policy documents of the C20, the following are recalled:

(a) 'Microsign', an enterprise in Bhavnagar, Gujarat, which is a successful example of how differently-abled persons are sought after and constitute preferred staff. Its 60 per cent workforce is differently-abled as preferred human resources. Even the *Harvard Business Review* mentions it in its publication of 16 March 2016, based on a study of IIM Ahmedabad.

(b) We also recalled Amrita Yuva Dharma Dhara (AYUDH), which denoted 'youth who perpetuate the wheel of *dharma* (righteousness)'. Stretching across Europe, North America, Asia, Australia, and Africa AYUDH empowered young people by integrating universal values into their daily lives. It aims to use the powerful force of young people to perpetuate harmony with Nature, social justice, and personal empowerment.

(c) A unique example of SEWA or self-help is *Halma*, an age-old self-help practice in the Bhil tribal community in the Jhabua district of Madhya Pradesh state in India where an entire village goes to the help of distressed families. Every year, thousands of tribal villagers come with the equipment needed for manual earthwork. They prepare contour trenches on hills, and dig pits for plantation. All this is for the community as a whole and not for any individual benefit. This effort has shown significant change on the ground in the form of improved water availability.

(d) *LIVE-IN-LABS*, which was established in 2013 in India, is a multidisciplinary international experiential learning programme that facilitates the research, development, and deployment of sustainable solutions for current challenges faced by rural communities in India.

The programme covers over 160 projects in 22 states across India and has touched the lives of approximately 600,000 rural residents. With participation from over 30 institutions around the world, it is a unique mutual learning and sharing experience in the field of education that breaks classroom and lab barriers to implement theoretical knowledge to address real-world problems.

(e) There was the long-standing inspirational example of the revival of the Aravari Basin in Rajasthan, India, where the river had dried after excess groundwater withdrawal and extraction in 1985. In response, the local community was mobilised to build structures for water retention and route rainwater using traditional harvesting systems and achieve increased water levels in wells and groundwater recharge due to less extraction. An *Aravari Sansad* or farmer's parliament was formed to establish community-led ownership of the river. Similar inspirational examples of cooperation for sustainable development have also been seen in the Mekong River Basin System of Southeast Asia, where the world's 12th-longest river running through six riparian countries had suffered due to continued regional conflict and geo-political barriers, leaving no structures on the Lower Mekong mainstream However, the Mekong Agreement that was signed amongst the Lower Mekong River Basin States (LMRBS) – Cambodia, Laos, Thailand and Vietnam – in 1995made major progress with water allocation.

(f) A major example of grassroots innovation is the *Palle Srujana* volunteer group based in Hyderabad, India, dedicated to enhancing the condition of grassroots innovators. *Palle Srujana* undertakes *shodh yatras* (search expeditions) to identify and document innovators. After identifying the innovator, it supports the technical improvement of the raw innovation, validation and patenting. So far *Palle Srujana* has identified about 78 innovators, and more than 1,000 traditional practices and registered them with the National Innovation Foundation. Three innovators have received national awards for their innovations. *Palle Srujana* runs purely on a volunteer basis. Dedicated volunteers who are passionate about grassroots innovations and have immense compassion for grassroots innovators are key to the work of *Palle Srujana*.

(g) Another successful example of intervention is the CRPF Gender Conversation training programme, designed and implemented by

Amrita University for India's para-military and police forces (CRPF). This programme addresses the issue of gender equality, masculinity, and mental health at the individual, household, and community levels to promote the well-being of CRPF servicemen and their families, and improve their overall morale. This is a unique programme that involves awareness building and training to encourage healthy dialogue on gender and mental health among the CRPF personnel and their families. It also seeks to promote them as positive role models at the community level.

Compassion: Desideratum for a Harmonious and Flourishing Future

The world is witnessing an alarming rise in violence against both humanity and the environment. Interpersonal violence affects millions of people with a staggering number of annual fatalities globally. While efforts are being made to address its causes, that alone is inadequate to restore peace and harmony in society and nature. The C20 Chair, Mata Amritanandamayi Devi, says: "People experience two types of poverty in this world – poverty of material goods and poverty of love and compassion". Compassion is the most important factor that can transform lives. It helps people to make decisions and actions with spontaneity, power and effect. As a foundational element, it will need to be integrated into our educational curriculum. It must instill a sense of oneness among individuals, amplifying their power to fight against odds and enabling them to live in harmony with nature for not just a sustainable but a flourishing future. We must strive to foster peace and harmony across continents, integrating cultural values and rediscovering local traditions.

Within India, an exemplary compassion practice developed recently is the geo-enabled software platform titled: 'Sustainability and Resilience for Community Engagement and Empowerment (SREE)' integrated with a crowd-sourced mobile application titled 'Empower Community.' This integrated platform is capable of measuring, mapping, analysing, and proposing recommendations for community-level sustainability and resilience indicators. SREE operates on community-driven data that is aggregated according to thematic layers which can be assessed on a multiscale approach bringing multiple stakeholders to a common knowledge acquisition level to make informed community decisions and resolve community-level sustainability and resilience assessment challenges. It has already been implemented in several countries in a participatory manner.

In its policy pack, the C20 observed that the world views of civil society organisations in various countries could naturally be expected to evolve along with the ethos of their respective communities and naturally reflect the civilisational values and principles of their respective societies. Against this backdrop, three policy briefs, in particular, were prepared by the Indian working groups, namely, those on *Sewa*, Lifestyle for Environment or LiFE, and *Vasudhaiva Kutumbakam* reflected the world view as well as the ethos essentially of civil society organisations from India, the host country. Despite their particularities and references to Indian conditions, briefs on these themes were included in the policy pack with a view to generating a larger conversation in the interests of the global community.

These are some of the significant contributions that the working groups set up under the Indian Chair of the C20 have made towards a more compassionate and caring world. It is most reassuring to see that under the G20 presidency of India, there was a fresh appreciation of the immense value and contribution being made by national as well as global civil society organisations. The Chair of the C20, Mata Amritanandamayi Devi or '*Amma*,' has been the driving force behind these unprecedented achievements, and stands as an iconic symbol of the theme of compassion. As a woman originating from a fishing community, not belonging to an educated elite, she has been representing the voices of the most marginalised and guiding the transformation of the lives of common people around the entire world today.

Inclusive Development and G20: Progress and Prospects

NITYA MOHAN KHEMKA

The aspiration towards inclusive development is grounded in South Asian tradition and thought. Mahatma Gandhi's emphasis on uplifting the village economy as a strategy for development as well as the dangers of unchecked growth and environmental degradation have formed the bedrock of the sustainability movement in much of South Asia.

Inclusive development refers to economic growth that extends benefits to the widest range of people, including the marginalised and vulnerable sections of society. It emphasises equal opportunities in terms of access to markets, resources, and an unbiased regulatory environment. It seeks to reduce inequalities, foster social harmony, and ensure that no one is left behind in the development process. This is consistent with Prime Minister Modi's credo of 'Sabka Saath, Sabka *Vikas*, Sabka Vishwas' (Participation of All, Development for All, Trust for All).

India's G20 presidency, culminating in the September 2023 New Delhi summit, was ground-breaking and transformative, shaping an inclusive world order amidst global challenges. Embracing the Vedic ethos of 'Vasudhaiva Kutumbakam,' it steered away from crisis and conflict, emphasising healing, hope, and harmony. Internationally lauded, it revitalised multilateralism, and its presidency will provide lessons for future presidencies, particularly from the Global South, as Brazil and South Africa take the helm in 2024-2025.

India's presidency of the G20 focused on six priorities which are green development, inclusive growth, progress on the United Nations sustainable development goals (SDGs), technological transformation, multilateral institutions for the 21st century, and women-led development. India stamped its vision of inclusive growth by emboldening its vision of *'One Earth One Family ·One Future'* through the theme of the Delhi Declaration at the G20 Delhi Summit.

Synergies between Health and Education

For inclusive development, education and healthcare must be viewed synergistically. Better education leads to improved health outcomes, as educated individuals are more likely to understand and access healthcare services. Conversely, a healthy population is better able to participate in and benefit from educational opportunities. Programs that address the health and nutrition of school-going children, such as the Midday Meal Scheme, which is a multi-faceted programme of the Government of India that seeks to tackle issues of food security, lack of nutrition, and access to education on a nationwide scale, exemplify this synergy.

Role of Education

India has made significant progress in improving access to quality education, increasing school enrolment, and reducing the number of out-of-school children. These achievements have been strengthened by key legislations, policies, and schemes such as the Right of Children to Free and Compulsory Education (RTE) Act (2009) which mandates eight years of quality education for all children aged 6-14; the Sarva Shiksha Abhiyan (SSA) which complements the RTE by aiming to universalise elementary education, bridging social, regional, and gender gaps; the National Early Childhood Care and Education (ECCE) Policy (2013); the Rashtriya Uchchatar Shiksha Abhiyan (RUSA) which seeks to boost the quality of state institutions; and the National Education Policy (2020), a transformative policy designed to overhaul India's education system. Recognising that formal education might not be the only path to employment, India has also emphasised vocational training through schemes like the Pradhan Mantri Kaushal Vikas Yojana (PMKVY).

However, while policies abound, the implementation often witnesses disparities. Fragmented service delivery, bureaucratic delays, inadequate infrastructure, and lack of awareness among beneficiaries can impede progress. Lessons from the pandemic have also shown that making education more accessible through online platforms and digital tools can help advance learning outcomes and bridge the rural-urban divide.

The G20 New Delhi Declaration portrayed its commitment to fostering quality and inclusive education in G20 member-nations through the 'Delivering Quality Education' goal that it identified in the declaration. The commitment revolves around promoting inclusive and high-quality education, with a specific focus on vulnerable groups. Recognising the foundational importance of literacy, numeracy, and socio-emotional skills, the emphasis was laid on their critical role in both education and employment. The pledge extends to leveraging digital technologies for overcoming disparities, providing support to educational institutions and teachers to adapt to emerging trends, including advancements in artificial intelligence.

Healthcare: Sustained Inclusive Development

India's healthcare system is characterised by a vast network of health facilities. Recent policy interventions have been focused on trying to improve the accessibility, affordability, and quality of healthcare services, particularly in rural areas. These include the National Health Mission (NHM) which aims to improve healthcare services by focusing on 18 states that have poor public health indicators and/or weak infrastructure; the Ayushman Bharat Scheme (2018), an ambitious initiative that aims to provide free healthcare coverage to over 500 million people, making it the world's largest government-sponsored healthcare scheme; the Pradhan Mantri Jan Arogya Yojana (PMJAY) which provides insurance cover for over 100 million vulnerable families; the Janani Suraksha Yojana (JSY) which incentivises institutional deliveries; and the Integrated Child Development Services (ICDS) program that focuses on holistic child development. These policies have contributed a great deal towards improving the inclusivity of healthcare delivery in India.

India's health goals within the G20 include fostering global cooperation to prevent future pandemics and enhance pandemic response coordination. Emphasising the development, manufacturing, and equitable delivery of medical countermeasures like vaccines and medicines, India advocates a robust supply chain integration. Furthermore, India aims to strengthen the 'One Health' initiative, combat antimicrobial resistance, and ensure universal access to healthcare, viewing them as vital components of pandemic preparedness and essential for comprehensive economic and social development. The endorsement of enhanced access to universal care and support for health innovations, including digital health applications such as AI and telemedicine, are key elements in India's approach, along with promoting data sharing and interoperability across G20 nations.

India also underscored specific health priorities, including the eradication of tuberculosis, mitigation of non-communicable diseases, and the integration of traditional medicine such as Ayurveda, into global health systems. By advocating for these initiatives, India seeks to contribute to a comprehensive and inclusive approach to global health within the G20 framework.

However, several challenges remain with the delivery of healthcare. For instance, while insurance schemes have expanded access, the quality of care can vary. Overburdened public health systems, lack of specialists in rural areas, and out-of-pocket expenditures remain pressing issues. The shortage of trained healthcare professionals is a major challenge. Incentivising medical education and facilitating the deployment of healthcare workers in underserved areas is essential.

Lessons for the World

India assumed the year-long presidency of G20 in December 2022. Under its presidency, there has been a significant emphasis on pushing for inclusive development as a cornerstone of the global agenda. Given the complex and interconnected challenges facing the world today – from economic inequality to climate change – leading such an influential group of countries has offered India a platform to drive meaningful change. India has vast experience in addressing challenges of poverty, innovation, and sustainability, and as G20 member-states positioned themselves to tackle these urgent issues at the G20 Summit in New Delhi, India leveraged its own experience to promote inclusive development in various ways.

India adopted an inclusive approach in its domestic handling of the G20, framing it as a People's Presidency in line with the principles of the world's largest democracy. Utilising *Jan Bhagidari* (people's participation) events, the G20 engaged with 1.4 billion citizens, collaborating with all states and Union Territories (UTs) as partners. Substantively, India steered international focus towards broader developmental goals, aligning its efforts with the mandate of the G20. In a step towards pursuing further inclusivity in development and progress, a principle that has characterised India since the Nehruvian era, the African Union, comprising 55 member-states, gained permanent G20 membership along with the European Union. This boosts Global South representation, and counters the long-standing dominance of G7 nations in the group.

In the field of health, concerning global health security in the wake of the COVID-19 pandemic, India has been leading discussions and actions to strengthen global preparedness for future pandemics, emphasising the importance of healthcare infrastructure and rapid response systems. It has used the platform to improve international cooperation for future pandemic preparedness, including vaccine development, manufacturing and distribution. India has also made strides in providing affordable healthcare solutions and brought this experience to the G20 table. The country's pharmaceutical sector has also been a major global player, providing affordable medications and vaccines. India's emphasis on cost-effective healthcare solutions can provide a blueprint for nations looking to optimise healthcare expenditure without compromising on quality.

Finally, leveraging its advancements in digital infrastructure, India is spearheading digital health initiatives that enable telemedicine, healthcare data analytics, and online health services to reach underserved populations. In this regard, India aimed to create a platform for sharing digital health innovations and solutions, exemplified by initiatives like CoWIN and e-Sanjeevani, to achieve better and universal health coverage. India championed the development of the Global Initiative on Digital Health

(GIDH) under the World Health Organisation (WHO). GIDH encompasses an investment tracker, a repository of digital health solutions, knowledge-sharing mechanisms, and an ask tracker to monitor the specific needs of different countries. While the proposal for a $ 200 million fund for a digital health program did not secure consensus, India committed to offer its digital platforms, including CoWIN and e-Sanjeevani, as global public goods.

India has also underscored the importance of inclusive and quality education as a means to foster sustainable development and economic growth. Education is central to the achievement of multiple Sustainable Development Goals (SDGs). India used its presidency to reiterate the importance of education in meeting these global goals, sharing strategies for effective implementation and monitoring. With the advent of digital technology in education, India has stressed the importance of digital literacy as a fundamental skill and discussed initiatives to provide accessible and affordable digital tools for education.

The 'G20 New Delhi Leaders' Declaration: Delivering Quality Education' with its purpose to revolutionise the education system, highlighted the pivotal role of foundational learning, including literacy, numeracy, and socio-emotional skills, as the primary building block for both education and employment. Additionally, the leaders reaffirmed their commitment to addressing the digital divide by harnessing digital technologies and supporting educational institutions and teachers to adapt to emerging trends, including advancements in AI. This included emphasising expanding access to high-quality Technical and Vocational Education and Training (TVET), promoting open and equitable scientific collaboration, and encouraging mobility across educational institutions. Lastly, a strong emphasis is placed on enabling lifelong learning, particularly focused on skilling, reskilling, and upskilling, with specific consideration for vulnerable groups.

India's focus on education, epitomized by campaigns like 'Beti Bachao, Beti Padhao' (Save the Daughter, Educate the Daughter), and innovations like the National Digital Library, offer lessons in using limited resources to achieve expansive goals. Finally, given the changing nature of the global job market, India promoted skill-based education and vocational training as a key agenda item, sharing its own experiences and programs like the Skill India initiative.

The Delhi summit recognised that achieving sustainability requires a holistic approach, and India's emphasis on community involvement in initiatives like the Clean India Mission highlighted the role of citizens in driving environmental change. The principles of 'sustainable living' and 'clean energy for all' emerged as shared aspirations for a greener future. India's model of leveraging private-sector collaboration for public welfare gained recognition. The summit discussions delved into how nations can encourage innovation, technological adoption, and collaboration with the private sector to accelerate inclusive growth. India's emphasis on affordable and accessible digital solutions served as a blueprint for others striving to bridge the digital divide.

Development Journey

India's socio-economic landscape is diverse and complex, but the country's commitment to inclusive development, especially in education and healthcare, is unwavering. The recent policy initiatives in India show a strong commitment towards achieving inclusive development. However, effective and efficient implementation of these policies is key. This requires relentless political will, increased financial allocations, robust data systems for monitoring progress, and active participation of civil society in holding the system accountable.

In an increasingly interconnected world, India's development journey holds lessons for many other nations striving to grow inclusively and sustainably. Today, as India successfully straddles the intersection of modernity and tradition, and is poised to become a USD 5 trillion economy, public-private partnerships, technology integration, community involvement, and robust monitoring mechanisms can fast-track the journey towards an inclusive and prosperous India. While challenges persist, the drive for inclusive development in India – by ensuring equitable access to quality education and healthcare – is a testament to the nation's vision for a sustainable, equitable and inclusive future.

India's experience and perspectives offer a rich source of insights into global challenges. As a key player in the G20, India not only stands to benefit from international cooperation but has also much to offer in shaping a more equitable and sustainable world order.

India plays a pivotal role in navigating global shifts, particularly amidst the impactful digital and climate transformations. Proactive engagement by India becomes crucial in steering actionable change for a sustainable and resilient future. Leveraging the implementation of sustainable development goals, India stands to unlock significant socio-economic benefits, including job creation, improved energy access, and heightened economic growth. The country has already demonstrated progress in clean energy, witnessing an 81 per cent increase in green jobs by January 2023. India's sustainability efforts extend across various fronts, emphasising the need for a paradigm shift where profitable economic activities inherently embody sustainable practices.

Three key catalysts for this transformative journey include the crucial role of technology in driving sustainable solutions, the necessity for global collaboration and collective action to address climate change, and the importance of raising awareness and driving education for widespread adoption of sustainable practices. India's government initiatives, such as the Global Biofuels Alliance with Brazil and the USA, the Green Skill Development Programme, and the Green Credits Programme, underscore the commitment to global cooperation and a greener future. As a key player in the G20, India not only stands to benefit from international cooperation but has also much to offer in shaping a more equitable and sustainable world order.

26

A Multipolar World: Forging G20 Unity to Accelerate UN Reforms and SDGs

ANNA-KATHARINA HORNIDGE AND ALMA WISSKIRCHEN

Can a multipolar world effectively confront the challenges posed by global conflict, the pervasive debt trap, and the natural disasters caused by global warming? Anna-Katharina Hornidge and Alma Wisskirchen describe the challenges ahead and explore how India can accelerate SDGs and promote green growth in the context of its G20 presidency.

July 2023 was the hottest month recorded to date. More than 830,000 hectares were burned within the territory of the European Union alone (not counting the devastating effects of wild fires in Canada, Russia, or the US), while China experienced in August the heaviest rainfall in the last 140 years. The extreme weather events of the past months are just some examples of the destructive effects of climate change and provide a glimpse of what to expect if global temperatures continue to rise. Meanwhile, approaching its midpoint, the implementation of the 2030 Agenda is alarmingly off-track: at the current rate of progress, only 18% of the Sustainable Development Goals (SDGs) will be implemented by 2030, and while 575 million people might still live in extreme poverty, more than 600 million could face hunger by 2030. These developments cannot be blamed on the failure of individual governments, but are the result of increasingly dangerous risks unfolding out of the interplay between global warming, loss of biodiversity, and geopolitical tensions. At the same time, they underline the need for concerted efforts of the international community to develop and implement measures that limit the global temperature increase to 1.5 degrees Celsius and accelerate the implementation of the 2030 Agenda.

Moribund UN?

While the ramifications of today's global challenges become increasingly evident, we observe a concomitant polarisation of the established global order. The United Nations, which was called into life to maintain international peace and security while promoting social progress, is blocked. Its composition and structures no longer represent today's realities. As a result of the UN's failure to adequately respond to and address the aforementioned challenges, the systems of global governance are moving from universal structures that are open to all nation-states to exclusive forums that are based on specific country groups and focus on a selected range of topics. While some of these group-based formats have opened the yearly summits in most recent years by inviting additional countries as observers (i.e., the Group of 7), others extend full memberships. The most recent example is the expansion of the BRICS group. Formed in 2009 by Brazil, Russia, India, and China (with South Africa joining in 2010), it seeks to provide an alternative voice to the West. On the other hand, following Russia's attack on Ukraine, western democracies in general and the G7 in particular have demonstrated great unity. As the unipolar moment that has emerged and shaped global governance since the end of the cold war is coming to an end, the emergence of a multipolar structure raises the fundamental question whether this will be a multipolar world or a world of multiple orders. Can a multipolar world stand in constructive cooperation in the future, or are we increasingly on the path to destructive competition and a further fragmentation into multiple orders no longer brought together by a universal system of multilateralism as we find it in the United Nations?

Acknowledging the global and interdependent nature of the aforementioned global challenges, the international community must, by all means, try to prevent the realisation of the latter scenario. Instead, global leaders should step up their efforts, taking the 2030 Agenda and its principles of universality and indivisibility as common ground to advance and deepen multilateral cooperation. Against the background of a blocked

UN system, the G20 presents an increasingly important forum to assume responsibility and leadership in advancing coordination and cooperation on the issues of sustainable development and growth. Bringing together the world's most important industrialised and emerging economies, the G20 represents 80% of global GDP while also being responsible for 80% of global emissions. As a forum that has both G7 and (the founding) BRICS states as its members, it provides an important platform to enable and promote discussion and engagement, thus working against a further polarisation between the different groupings. A joint concentration on uniting convergences rather than divisive differences becomes possible.

One Earth and LiFE

The theme of India's G20 presidency "One Earth, One Family, One Future" illustrates the presidency's focus on the interconnected nature of human life, animals and plants, indicating the potential implications of human activity on our planet and common future. In line with this theme, the Indian presidency has prioritised the topics 'sustainable development' and 'just and equitable growth', advancing, among others, the concept of 'women-led development' and the 'LiFE approach'. This prioritisation constitutes an important and welcome initiative, as it could and should accelerate the G20 members' efforts to implement the 2030 Agenda. More concretely, at the G20 summit and for the remainder of its presidency, India should build on the ongoing discussions, using its position as the world's most populous country, the second largest emerging economy and (self-proclaimed) voice of the Global South to forge common ground and pave the way for the UN SDG Summit in New York. To make its presidency a success and to enable real progress on SDG implementation, the Indian presidency needs to advance the G20's work in three important areas: reform of the multilateral system, debt relief and the reform of the international financial architecture, and national SDG implementation.

Reform, Finance and SDGs

The first point, reform of the multilateral system stems, as elaborated above, from the UN's failure to adequately respond to global challenges and to be responsive to all its member states. The permanent members of the UN

Security Council neither represent today's global distributions of power nor are they representative in terms of population size. Notwithstanding these shortcomings, the UN system remains the most inclusive forum to provide global governance and can and must not be replaced by any exclusive group of states. Acknowledging the importance of the UN system, the G20 should accompany and foster discussions and concrete steps to make the reform of the UN system (including the UN Security Council) possible. In the meantime, however, the G20 becomes even more important to address key global issues and should thus seek to be more inclusive and effective. The Indian presidency's proposal to integrate the African Union (AU) as a permanent member into the group would strengthen the G20's representation and outreach. Bringing the AU to the G20 table would allow the G20 to directly engage with the representation of 55 African states. Hence, seeking to advance reforms on both the multilateral level and within the G20, India must use the remainder of its presidency to foster discussions on UN reforms and the integration of the AU into the G20.

A second major obstacle to SDG implementation is the lack of sufficient finance. In February 2023, UN Secretary General Antonio Guterres called for an SDG stimulus, underlining the need for new public and private finance for the 2030 Agenda. A large majority of low- and middle-income countries are in severe debt distress, paying higher amounts on debt service than on investing in their own countries and citizens. This weakens both their capacity to respond to extreme weather events and to advance national SDG implementation. As the G20 comprises the largest creditor nations, it is of fundamental importance to advance discussions on the issue of debt restructuring. In doing so, the G20 should consider innovative measures such as debt-for-climate swaps, which can be particularly effective when efforts are closely coordinated and directed towards a jointly identified set of countries. Finally, responding to Guterres' call for an SDG stimulus, G20 countries should mobilise new private and public finance to provide the required 500 billion USD per year.

As a third and last point, the G20 under India's presidency should prioritise national SDG implementation. The UN's Department of Economic and Social Affair's 2023 SDG report shows that countries of all income levels are not on track in implementing the 2030 Agenda. Additionally, policy incoherence and spillover effects hamper effective implementation. According to the International Energy Agency, renewable power capacity has to be tripled by 2030 to keep the global temperature increase to 1.5 degrees Celsius. Yet, while investments in renewable energies have increased, the G20 has recently drastically augmented consumer subsidies on fossil fuels. The fact that the outcome document of the third meeting of G20 energy ministers mentions neither phasing out of fossil fuels nor reducing fossil fuel subsidies demonstrates that much remains to be done on these issues. Similarly, spillover effects, which refer to the negative implications of progress in one sector or country on another sector or country, remain unaddressed in the outcome document of the G20 development ministers. If the G20 in general and the Indian presidency in particular want to advance sustainable development and SDG implementation, they have to show serious efforts in advancing these topics within their own countries. Looking at the G20 process so far, the Indian presidency has put great emphasis on advancing sustainable development and just and equitable growth. Against the backdrop of the recent BRICS expansion, mounting geopolitical tensions and the alarming mid-term review of the 2030 Agenda, India should use the remainder of its presidency to forge unity among the G20 and find common ground with regard to reforming the UN system and the international financial architecture as well as implementing the 2030 Agenda. By striving for unity, coordinated and concerted efforts to implement the SDGs, the G20 summit can pave the way for the UN SDG Summit in September. Just as important, the G20 can strengthen its role as a forum for sustainable development, counteracting current tendencies towards greater polarisation and destructive competition.

27

Integrating Cultural Outreach in G20

ABHAY K.

In a world that thrives on divisiveness, India showcased the spirit of oneness during its G20 presidency by upholding the ancient Indian philosophy of 'Vasudhaiva *Kutumbakam*' and its extension, 'One Earth, One Family, One Future'.

India's G20 presidency provided a one-of-a-kind opportunity to showcase the diversity and richness of Indian culture, heritage, art, and hospitality to the world's 20 largest economies and other invited guest countries.

Culture acts as a cohesive agent for growth and development in international relations. Two Indian philosophies, namely, '*Vasudhaiva Kutumbakam*' and '*Atithi Devo Bhava*', have always been part of Indian traditions and they were evident during multiple successful G20 meetings throughout the year across various Indian states and Union Territories.

India is home to a diverse range of songs, music, dance, theatre, tribal and folk traditions, performing and visual arts, rites and rituals, literature, and writings known as the 'Intangible Cultural Heritage' of humanity. Each Indian state boasts rich traditions and art forms.

From December 2022 to November 2023, over 60 Indian cities hosted various G20 meetings. The Indian Council for Cultural Relations (ICCR), in collaboration with respective state governments, was entrusted with the responsibility of organising cultural events for the visiting G20 delegates. More than 300 cultural programmes were organised in 139 G20 meetings in which over 17,000 artists from various parts of India performed.

Modus Operandi: How was it done?

The Indian Council of Cultural Relations (ICCR) was entrusted with the task of organising cultural events at various meetings during India's G20 presidency. In view of the importance of these high-profile events and in order to make them memorable for the foreign dignitaries, it was important to curate high-impact cultural events showcasing India's diversity, heritage, and culture through vibrant and enthralling performances.

The ICCR's mandate was to coordinate and ensure the high quality of cultural events. Indian states and Union Territories were to organise these cultural events with logistics support from the G20 Secretariat. They were offered the following five parameters to keep in mind while curating the cultural events. Cultural events should be:

1. Holistic and inclusive
2. Grassroot driven
3. Impactful and vibrant
4. Fast paced and rhythmic
5. Immersive and engaging.

A team was constituted at the ICCR with a programme director and a programme officer to initiate planning. Subsequently, consultants, junior consultants and office assistants were employed on a contractual basis. A joint secretary-rank officer of the Ministry of External Affairs was appointed as Deputy Director-General, ICCR, responsible for G20 cultural events, to lead the team.

To ensure smooth functioning and success, governments of the Indian States and Union Territories were approached to extend their support and collaboration to realise this prestigious undertaking.

The ICCR sought support from the governments of States or Union Territories for the following:

(i) Availability of, with required permissions, to use iconic sites suitable [or recommended] for organising cultural events
(ii) Providing performing groups, choreographers, etc., by the state cultural departments for participation in the cultural events
(iii) Traditional welcome for delegates (small cultural presentations at airport arrivals or at the meeting venues)

(iv) Ambience design at meeting venues, gala dinners, cultural events by showcasing and exhibiting artefacts, handicrafts, other items of décor, etc.

(v) To designate a nodal Officer for related coordination.

The proposals received from state governments were examined thoroughly, and required modifications were suggested after consultation and revision of event schedules. An expert committee at the ICCR consisting of distinguished people from various walks of life examined the proposals made by the various state governments/Union Territories.

The ICCR ensured the preparation of theme-based presentations, which largely involved the participation of local talent, and inclusion of more than one art form in the presentation, managed and vetted the technical requirements, that is, stage, lights, sound, etc. through the logistics vertical of the G20 Secretariat, engaged the master of ceremony, who was well versed in the respective state's culture and reviewed his/her script.

Types of Cultural Programmes/Presentations

(i) At the welcome dinner – a 20-minute instrumental or musical performance during the meal.

(ii) At the gala dinner/Samvaad over Dinner – It was the main cultural event during the meeting. A specially curated event before the meal followed by live music, showcasing the cultural heritage of the state concerned. The cultural programme consisted of small performances, as it was difficult to keep the audience engaged for a long time. It consisted of three to four performances, each of ten minutes duration, of a diverse nature woven together in an aesthetic manner by a professional choreographer engaged by the state/UT.

(iii) At the second dinner – This was a working dinner. About 20 minutes of a cultural programme was organised before the meal.

(vi) Filler performances/presentations – Before the inauguration of the meeting for a maximum duration of ten minutes, or some live music during lunch hour.

(v) Small welcome presentations at the airport.

The cultural events were aimed at showcasing the cultural heritage of the States/UTs concerned. The choreographers/artists were advised to adopt the following broad parameters while curating the performances: fast-paced and impactful, holistic and immersive with audience participation wherever feasible.

The state governments and UTs were directed to appoint a choreographer to curate the gala dinner cultural programmes. The appointment of choreographers was very important for the proper creation and coordination of the event and to ensure that various artistic elements in the cultural programme were tightly woven to create culturally aesthetic and appealing performances. The choreographer played a critical role in coordinating with the ICCR and with the event management company (EMC) on technical requirements for the events.

The participation of local artists was ensured for each cultural event so as to showcase local flavour. Many budding artists were also given the opportunity to perform during G20 cultural events.

The innovative compositions were curated on the themes identified by the state governments and UTs as well as the ambience design at meeting venues, gala dinners, cultural events with the live display of traditional arts and artefacts, handicrafts, and other items characteristic of the states and Union Territories.

All technical requirements for the cultural events, that is, stage, lights, sound, green rooms, etc., were taken care of by the G20 Secretariat through the designated EMC.

Thus, the ICCR played a key role in coordinating with stakeholders such as the State Government, EMC, Tourism Department, Security Department, and the G20 Secretariat by working with the State /UT Government to identify the appropriate cultural presentation for each meeting, collaborating with a team of dedicated nodal officers and field officers, assessing technical requirements, and managing the overall process to ensure the highest quality cultural experience and bringing out the best that the States/UTs had to offer in terms of musical and performing arts to showcase the state's culture.

Iconic sites or monuments were chosen as venues for cultural performances such as Manak Chowk at City Palace in Udaipur, and Gateway of India, Mumbai, among others. Most of the events were organised by the state channelling the local talents. All cultural events were successfully curated with elements of audience engagement which the foreign delegates enjoyed thoroughly.

During India's G20 presidency, cultural diplomacy fostered a better understanding and collaboration among the member-countries. Cultural events, exhibitions, and performances organised during G20 meetings created informal and convivial space for discussions and relationship-building.

India is known for its cultural diversity, including languages, traditions, art, and cuisines. The G20 presidency served as an opportunity for India to showcase this diversity and promote cross-cultural understanding among the member-countries.

India's G20 presidency has also facilitated collaboration between artists, musicians, writers, and filmmakers from different countries, promoting cross-cultural understanding and creative synergy.

India's cultural, creative, and tourism industries contribute significantly to its economy. During its G20 presidency, India has emphasised the economic potential of its cultural and tourism sectors and discussed how these sectors can be major forces for economic growth and job creation. By showcasing cultural landmarks, historical sites, and vibrant cities, India could attract more tourists, promoting its tourism sector.

India, during its G20 presidency, demonstrated its rich and diverse cultural treasures, which is a matter of pride for every citizen of this country.

Performing Arts

A series of classical, folk, and tribal dances and music reflected the multi-cultural, and pluralistic society of India. India's rich cultural tapestry is woven with an array of classical and folk dance forms, each a testament to the nation's artistic and traditional heritage. Among the illustrious classical dances are Kathak, Odissi, Manipuri, Sattriya, Kuchipudi, Bharata Natyam, Mohini Attam, and Kathakali. Recently, during the G20 meetings, these eight classical dance forms took centre stage, presenting India's cultural potpourri.

The G20 cultural extravaganza during India's presidency began at the 1st Sherpa meeting in Lake City Udaipur in Rajasthan on 4 December 2022. The first cultural performance was held at the stunning Jag Mandir Palace, which is located in the middle of the Pichola Lake in Udaipur. Guests arrived at the venue in specially decorated boats and were treated to sumptuous orchestral compositions of Rajasthani folk music to the accompaniment of classical instruments in the courtyard of Jag Mandir followed by a forty-minute memorable cultural performance titled 'Colours of Rajasthan' curated by Maitreyee Pahari, marking the inauguration of India's G20 presidency and showcasing Rajasthan's rich cultural heritage including Rajasthani folk dances like Ghoomar and Kalbeliya, among others. The guests also relished traditional Rajasthani cuisine such as bajra roti and gatta kadhi. On the second day, they were treated to a grand cultural performance titled 'Colours of India' featuring over 450 artists; some of them made a grand entry on camels and horses. The cultural performance included all the classical dance forms and 18 folk dance forms from various parts of India. A special laser projection and 3D digital mapping projection on the walls of the City Palace added to the grandeur of the cultural event. These two grand opening cultural performances set the tone for the rest of the cultural events during India's presidency of G20.

The captivating cultural performances throughout 2023 until September, underscored the nation's vibrant artistic legacy, with each dance form emanating its own unique flavour and narrative. Beyond the classical forms, the Indian states came alive with a plethora of folk dances, offering a window into the heart of each state's customs and ethos. For instance, the Lavani of Maharashtra, the spirited Bhangra and graceful Gidda of Punjab, the energetic Garba and Maniyaro of Gujarat, the Dollu Kunita and Veeragase of Karnataka, the Perini Natyam of Telangana, Kolattam of Andhra Pradesh, the vivacious Thira and Pulikali of Kerala and Poikkal Kutharai Attam of Tamilnadu, among others, collectively painted a vivid picture of regional diversity. The Bihu dance of Assam, including Mishing, Bodo, Dimasa, Karbi, Rabha and Hajong and the indigenous dance forms of Nagaland, Jharkhand, Manipur, and Arunachal Pradesh, further contributed to this colourful tapestry.

Every dance form is a living embodiment of the artistic finesse and cultural depth of the region. These artistic expressions collectively weave the fabric of India's cultural identity, offering a glimpse into the intricate tapestry of traditions and narratives that grace each state.

Amidst the grandeur of the G20 meetings, a symphony of captivating cultural performances tickled the senses of the delegates. The stage came alive with a harmonious blend of traditions as the attendees were enthralled by a medley of traditional and contemporary melodies, folkloric tunes, indigenous rhythms, and innovative fusions, meticulously orchestrated by well-known musicians.

The musical panorama presented a kaleidoscope of acoustic wonders, a testament to the vastness of India's musical heritage. These performances were not just harmonies; they were stories told through melodies, a cultural bridge connecting the past with the present. Among these renditions, the audience was treated to ethereal and rare instrumental music, transporting them to realms of sonic novelty. In this aural celebration, the delegates were given a glimpse of India's musical legacy, each note resonating with the essence of a thousand tales. The performances stood as a vibrant mosaic of cultural narratives, uniting tradition with innovation and leaving an indelible imprint on the collective memory of the G20 guests.

Visual Arts

Visual arts and artistic interpretation, inclusive of paintings, sculptures, art installations, and literature, considered valuable treasures of India, constitute a salient part of Indian culture. During the meetings of the G20 presidency, India presented art exhibitions of great masters, as well as folk traditions. The exhibits were not merely limited to the visual arts but included other artistic forms such as handlooms, rangoli, and handicrafts of various states. *Jal Sanjhi* presented in Rajasthan and Hyderabad was an epic example of art forms in water. Sand art and mandala art exhibited in Karnataka, Gujarat, and Ladakh were highly praised by the delegates of the G20 member-countries.

Contemporary and great artworks comprising paintings, sculptures, and multimedia installations were exhibited at some of the venues of the meetings. Artworks of some foremost Indian artists like Jaimini Roy, Rabindranath Tagore, Nandalal Bose, Subodh Gupta, M. F. Hussain, S. H. Raza, and Jayashree Burman were presented and exhibited.

Folk and tribal art like Madhubani, Warli, Phad, Kalamkari, etc., were also presented, featuring a diverse range of Indian traditional artworks exploring the vibrant range of colours, textures, and cultural symbolism unique to the country.

Heritage Sites

India is home to numerous UNESCO World Heritage Sites. The G20 presidency organised visits to some of these iconic sites, offering delegates the opportunity to experience India's rich architectural wonders firsthand. Cultural diplomacy is a unique way to further economic benefits for the state and boost tourism. In the excursions curated for the delegates, India was able to showcase both its architectural heritage as well as its diversity in landscapes.

The sites included a shikara ride in the iconic Dal Lake in Kashmir, the Loktak Lake in Manipur, the backwaters in Kerala, the Ajanta and Ellora Caves in Maharashtra, the Kumbhalgarh Fort in Rajasthan, the Sandbar Brahmaputra Islands in Assam, and the river cruise in Babughat in Kolkata, to name a few. Delegates even witnessed Ganga Aarti in Varanasi and Chapchar Kut (the harvest festival) in Mizoram.

The broad spectrum of heritage experiences included staying in Kutch's Tent City in Gujarat and visits to the temples at Mahabalipuram in Tamil Nadu, Khajuraho in Madhya Pradesh, and Konark in Odisha. The attendees witnessed a wide range of native flora and fauna from various parts of India, from the red panda and orchids in Sikkim to the coconut trees in the south. Even the majestic Himalayas, Bay of Bengal, and the Arabian Sea served as backdrops to numerous cultural events that highlighted the magnificence of our nation.

Gastronomy and Culture

Culinary experience is unquestionably an excellent navigator in understanding one's culture. The G20 events offered a culinary treat to the delegates with a wide range of mouth-watering regional dishes, taking them on a tour of India's diverse food culture. G20 delegates had the opportunity to relish Indian cuisine from various regions like Daal Baati and Churma from the deserts of Rajasthan, Makki di Roti and Sarson da saag from Punjab, fish-based curries from the coastal regions of the country and fermented bamboo dishes from Arunachal Pradesh.

The Year of the Millet was inculcated in the regional dishes showing its importance in Indian culinary traditions. Various cooking demonstrations and cultural evenings featuring traditional dishes of various seasons gave the delegates a taste of Indian culinary delights.

In the lead-up to the Heads of State Summit in New Delhi in September 2023, the Culture Ministers' Meeting was held in Varanasi, India on 26 August 2023. The 'Kashi Culture Pathway' was adopted by G20 Culture Ministers, under the following four broad priorities identified by the members:

1. Protection and Restitution of Cultural Property
2. Harnessing Living Heritage for a Sustainable Future
3. Promotion of Cultural and Creative Industries, and Creative Economy
4. Leveraging Digital Technologies for the Promotion and Protection of Culture

It also called for the following actions:

- Standing united against the destruction of cultural heritage
- Building a strengthened and effective global coalition to bolster the fight against illicit trafficking of cultural property
- Resolving issues and enabling the return and restitution of cultural property to their countries and communities of origin
- Strengthening institutional and policy frameworks to harness living heritage for sustainable development
- Stopping the misuse and misappropriation of living cultural

heritage, practices and cultural expressions, particularly of local communities as well as of indigenous peoples
- Enhancing cooperation and dialogue on strengthening and aligning conceptual and monitoring frameworks, including classification of cultural and creative sectors and industries and the creative economy
- Supporting policies that promote the contribution of those working in the culture, arts and heritage sectors
- Strengthening and adapting cultural policy and legal frameworks to encompass digital technologies to safeguard intellectual property, notably as regards the digitalisation of living cultural heritage of local communities and indigenous peoples
- Continuing dialogue and exchange of expertise on climate action across the culture work stream as a critical cross-cutting issue striving towards environmental sustainability, notably by joining efforts to protect and safeguard the world's cultural and natural heritage from the impact of climate change
- Integrating culture and the creative economy into the development processes and policies

On 9 September 2023, the Group of 20 adopted a Leaders' Declaration during the 18th Heads of State and Government Summit, in which culture was kept at the centre for stronger sustainable development policy commitment by the G20 members.

Under a paragraph titled 'Culture as a Transformative Driver of SDGs', G20 members recognised the vital role of culture in achieving global Sustainable Development Goals:

> "We call for the full recognition and protection of culture with its intrinsic value as a transformative driver and an enabler for the achievement of the SDGs and advance the inclusion of culture as a standalone goal in future discussions on a possible post-2030 development agenda. We reiterate our commitment to strengthen our fight against illicit trafficking of cultural property at national, regional or international levels to enable its return and restitution to their countries and communities of origin as relevant, and call for sustained dialogue and action in that endeavour with a view to

strengthen cultural diplomacy and intercultural exchanges, consistent with national law and relevant UNESCO Conventions. We encourage the international community to protect the living cultural heritage, including the intellectual property, notably with regard to the impact of the over-commercialisation and misappropriation of such living heritage on the sustainability and on the livelihoods of practitioners and community bearers as well as indigenous peoples."

India's presidency of the G20 provided it with a platform to showcase a wide spectrum of Indian culture and India as a premium destination for tourism. It was for the first time that G20 events were hosted in each and every state and Union Territory of India, providing each of them with the opportunity to showcase the best of their culture. India's G20 presidency has emerged as a source of national pride, with India demonstrating the richness and diversity of its culture to an international audience and thus projecting its soft power globally.

About the Contributors

Dr. G.N.M. Pandor is South Africa's Minister of International Relations and Cooperation. Before this, she served as the Minister of Higher Education and Training (2018 to 2019), Minister of Science and Technology (2014 to 2018), Minister of Home Affairs (2012 to 2014), Minister of Science and Technology (2009 to 2012) and Minister of Education (2004 to 2009). She's been a Member of Parliament since 1994. Dr. Pandor has a PhD from the University of Pretoria (2019) and holds honorary doctorates from Cape Peninsula University of Technology, University of Stellenbosch, University of Lisbon, Portugal, and University College Dublin, Ireland.

Amitabh Kant is India's G20 Sherpa. He was CEO, NITI Aayog (National Institution for Transforming India), India's premier policy think tank. Prior to that, Kant, an Indian Administrative Service officer, served as Secretary, Department of Industrial Policy & Promotion. He is the author of *Branding India – An Incredible Story, Incredible India 2.0* and has edited The *Path Ahead: Transformative Ideas for India.* He has been a key driver of 'Make in India', 'Startup India,' 'Incredible India' and 'God's Own Country' initiatives which positioned and branded India and Kerala as leading manufacturing and tourism destinations.

Harsh Vardhan Shringla is the Chief Coordinator of India's G20 Presidency. Prior to this, he was the Foreign Secretary of India. In a four-decade long Indian Foreign Service career, he has been Ambassador to the United States of America, Bangladesh and Thailand. He was Consul-General of India in Durban, South Africa, and Ho Chi Minh City, Vietnam. He is also an experienced multilateral diplomat, having worked on two UN Security Council tenures, served in the Indian Mission to the UN in New York and as Permanent Representative to UNESCAP.

Muktesh K. Pardeshi currently serves as Secretary (Consular, Passport, Visa and Overseas Indian Affairs) in the Ministry of External Affairs, New Delhi. In his current role, he also oversees India's relations with the Gulf and West Asia & North Africa (WANA) regions. He has successfully led the operations and organization of India's G20 Presidency Secretariat as Special Secretary since July 2022 and earlier served as the Chief Passport Officer of India. Between July 2019 and July 2022, he served as the High Commissioner of India to New Zealand. He was the Ambassador of India to Mexico from April 2016 to June 2019.

H.E. Vincenzo de Luca was appointed as the Ambassador of Italy to India on 18 December 2019 and Ambassador of Italy to Nepal on 22 October 2021. Previously, he was Director-General for the Promotion of the Country System from 1 February 2016, after having served in the same Directorate-General in the position of Deputy General Manager and Central Director for the internationalization of the Country System and territorial autonomies (since January 2014). He entered diplomatic service in Italy in 1989 and has held various positions at the Ministry of Foreign Affairs and at the diplomatic missions of Khartoum, Tunis, Paris (at the Permanent Mission to the O.C.S.E.) and Shanghai.

H.E. Kenneth Félix Haczynski da Nóbrega is the Ambassador of Brazil to India and Bhutan. In his diplomatic career, Ambassador Haczynski da Nóbrega has held several positions at the Ministry of Foreign Affairs, which include, among others, Secretary for Europe, Middle East and Africa 2019-03/2023); Director of Interregional Mechanisms (2016-2018), and BRICS and IBSA Sous-Sherpa; Trade Policy Advisor to the foreign minister's office (2013-2015). His diplomatic assignments abroad include stints in Washington, Berlin and Lima. He has also taken part in several inter-agency groups, including the Inter-ministerial Group of Intellectual Property at the Chamber of Foreign Trade, as Deputy Representative (2008-2011) and Permanent Representative (2011-2013), and the Counter-Piracy National Council, as Deputy Representative (2008-2013). He speaks Portuguese, English, French, Spanish, Polish and German.

Prof. Nagesh Kumar is Director of the Institute for Studies in Industrial Development (ISID), a New Delhi-based policy think-tank. He has served as Director at UNESCAP, Bangkok, from 2009-2021. During 2002-2009, Prof. Kumar served as the Director-General of the Research and Information System for Developing Countries (RIS). He has served as a consultant for the World Bank among other international organizations. He has authored 18 books and over 120 peer-reviewed papers.

Anil Sooklal is Ambassador-at-Large for Asia and BRICS, Department of International Relations and Cooperation, South Africa. He serves as South Africa's BRICS Sherpa, IBSA (India, Brazil, South Africa) Sherpa and Indian Ocean Rim Association Focal Point. He previously served as South Africa's G20 Sherpa and as Ambassador to the European Union, Belgium, and Luxembourg. He has been conferred a slew of awards and honours, including Pravasi Bharatiya Divas Samman (Government of India, 2019) and Order of Friendship, Russian Federation (2024). He is Extraordinary Professor, North West University, South Africa; Senior Adjunct Research Fellow, RIS, New Delhi, and member of the International Advisory Board, South African Institute of International Affairs (SAIIA). He is a Distinguished Advisor to India and the World Journal and Centre for Global India Insights, a think tank based on global affairs.

Sujan Chinoy is the Director-General of the Manohar Parrikar Institute for Defence Studies and Analyses (MP-IDSA), New Delhi, since 2019. He was the Chair of the Think20 engagement group for India's G20 presidency. A career diplomat from 1981 to 2018, he held several important diplomatic assignments, including as Ambassador to Japan. He is a specialist on China, East Asia and politico-military and security issues. On deputation to the National Security Council Secretariat (NSCS) from 2008 to 2012, his expertise covered external and internal security issues including the extended neighbourhood of the Indo-Pacific. He has served as Consul-General in Shanghai and Sydney and has extensive experience in trade, investment and economic issues. He regularly contributes to newspapers and journals, besides lecturing in India and overseas.

Vijay K. Nambiar served as India's Permanent Representative to the UN in New York. He was the Principal Coordinator, Civil Society 20 (C20) engagement group under India's G20 presidency. He joined the Indian Foreign Service in 1967. Subsequently, he served as India's Ambassador/

High Commissioner in Afghanistan (1990-1992), Malaysia (1993-1996), China (1996-2000) and Pakistan (2000-2001). Post-retirement, he served as Deputy National Security Adviser of India (2004-2006). He was then deputed by the Government of India to serve in the United Nations Secretariat as Under Secretary-General, Special Adviser to Secretary-General Kofi Annan (2006-2007), then as Chef de Cabinet to Secretary-General Ban Ki-moon (2007-2012) and later as Adviser on Myanmar (2012-2016).

Lakshmi Puri is former Indian Ambassador, United Nations Assistant Secretary-General and founding Deputy Executive Director of first global organization for Gender Equality and Women's Empowerment – UNWOMEN. She has actively engaged in multilateral diplomacy since 1981. She has held leadership positions at the United Nations for 15 years including as Director, International Trade Division, UNCTAD. She is a Distinguished Fellow of the Indian Association of International Studies (IAIS) and a recipient of the prestigious Eleanor Roosevelt Prize for Human Rights. She is the author of the much-acclaimed novel *Swallowing the Sun*.

Mohan Kumar spent 36 years in the Indian Foreign Service culminating in being India's Ambassador to France. He is currently Dean and Professor at OP Jindal Global University and is the Director of the G20 Centre there. He is the author of the much-acclaimed book, *India's Moment: Changing Power Equations around the World*. He has enormous expertise in the area of international trade; he was India's lead negotiator first at the GATT (General Agreement on Tariffs and Trade) and then at the WTO (World Trade Organization) in crucial areas such as Intellectual Property Rights, Services, Dispute Settlement, Rules and Technical Barriers to Trade. He is the author of a book titled *Negotiation Dynamics of the WTO: An Insider's Account*.

Dr. Arvind Gupta is the Director of the Vivekananda International Foundation, New Delhi. He was the Deputy National Security Adviser and Secretary, National Security Council, Government of India during 2014-17. Earlier, he was Director-General of the Institute for Defence Studies and Analyses, Ministry of Defence, New Delhi, during 2012-2014 and a former career diplomat. He has served in the Ministry of External Affairs and Indian missions abroad. He is the author of many books, including *Opportunity for India in a Changing World*, and *How India Manages Its National Security*. He has co-edited (with Anil Wadhwa) a volume titled *India's Foreign Policy: Surviving in a Turbulent World*; co-edited with Arpita Mitra, a volume titled *Vasudhaiva Kutumbakam: The Relevance of India's Ancient Thinking to Contemporary Strategic Reality*.

Dr. Mukesh Aghi is the President and Chief Executive Officer of the US-India Strategic Partnership Forum. In his current role, he works extensively with business and government leaders in the USA and India to promote trade and strengthen ties between the two countries. He has over 20 years of success in powering business expansion globally, boosting revenue, and increasing margins for companies in a variety of sectors. Previously, he served as Chief Executive and Member of the Board at L&T Infotech. He was recognized by *Esquire* magazine as a Global Leader and has won many awards over the course of his professional career, including the J. R. D. Tata Leadership Award. Most recently, He was the recipient of the Pravasi Bharatiya Samman Award.

D.B. Venkatesh Varma is Distinguished Fellow, Vivekananda International Foundation, and Co-Chair of the Think7 Task Force on Multilateralism in the Think Twenty (T20) Engagement Group. During his diplomatic career, he has worked in the Ministry of External Affairs, in the Office of the External Affairs Minister and in the Prime Minister's Office. He served as India's Ambassador to the Conference on Disarmament in Geneva, to the Kingdom of Spain and to the Russian Federation until October 2021. He has vast experience in India's security and defence policies, including its nuclear, missile, and space programs. He was a key member of the Indian negotiating team involved in the Civil Nuclear Initiative with the USA during his tenure as Director in the Prime Minister's Office during 2004-2007, and as a member of the Indian delegation to the Conference on Disarmament and as Joint Secretary in the Ministry of External Affairs.

Pradeep S. Mehta is the founder Secretary-General of the Jaipur-based Consumer Unity & Trust Society (CUTS International), a global economic policy research, advocacy and networking NGO established in 1983 in India, with centres in Nairobi, Lusaka, Hanoi, Accra, Geneva and Washington DC. Currently he is a member of the WTO DG's NGO

Advisory Board for the third time. He also serves on the G20/B20's Council on Africa's Economic Integration. He has been conferred the prestigious *Business World* Social Impact Award.

Anna-Katharina Hornidge is director of the German Institute of Development and Sustainability (IDOS) and Professor for Global Sustainable Development at the University of Bonn. She served as Professor of Social Sciences in the Marine Tropics at the University of Bremen and Head of Department, 'Social Sciences' and the research group 'Development and Knowledge Sociology' at the Leibniz Centre for Tropical Marine Research (ZMT) in Bremen. In her research, she focuses on the role of different types of knowledge in and for processes of change and questions of natural resources governance in agricultural and marine contexts. Her regional focus lies on the Southeast and Central Asia, West and East Africa.

Gurjit Singh is former Ambassador of India to Germany, Indonesia, Ethiopia, ASEAN and the African Union. He Chaired the CII Business Task Force on Trilateral Cooperation in Africa including the Asia-Africa Growth Corridor with Japan. He comments on current events on TV and in journals. His report on such cooperation in 2019 focused on private sector engagement to make trilaterals successful. He is associated with the social impact investment movement and is working on expanding it in Africa along with other trilateral initiatives, including with Japan, for B2B engagement. He is an independent director of companies achieving social impact. He is also associated with civil society efforts through the Aavishkar Foundation, and the Advisory Council of Nobel Peace Laureate, Kailash Satyarthi.

Elizabeth Sidiropoulos is the chief executive of the South African Institute of International Affairs (SAIIA), an independent foreign policy think-tank based in Johannesburg. She has headed the Institute since 2005. Earlier, she was research director at the South African Institute of Race Relations and editor of the highly acclaimed Race Relations Survey (now the *South Africa Survey*), an annual publication documenting political and constitutional developments, and socio-economic disparities in South Africa. She is a member of the International Advisory Board of the Indian *Foreign Affairs* Journal, the journal of the Graduate Institute of International

Development in Geneva and the International Journal *Chinese Quarterly of Strategic Studies* under the Shanghai Institute for International Studies (SIIS). She is the editor-in-chief of the South African *Journal of International Affairs*. Her expertise lies in South Africa's foreign policy, South-South cooperation and the role of emerging powers in Africa.

Manish Chand is Founder-CEO *India Writes Network* (www.india writes.org) and Centre for Global India Insights (CGII), a think tank, which focuses on India's burgeoning global engagements. He is Editor-in-Chief, I*ndia and The World*, an influential magazine-journal focused on international affairs. A veteran journalist and foreign policy analyst, he has edited three special editions of *India and the World* journal on India's G20 presidency. He has edited several publications and books, including '*Journeys Across Continents: A New India on the Global Stage*'" the first-of-its-kind book that maps PM Modi's journeys to various foreign countries. He is the Editor of the much-acclaimed book on India-Africa relations, titled '*Two Billion Dreams: Celebrating India-Africa Friendship*'. He is a co-editor of '*India-Africa Partnership: Towards Sustainable Development*' and co-editor of '*Engaging with Resurgent Africa*'" (published by Macmillan). He was Editor of *Africa Quarterly*, a prestigious journal focused on India-Africa relations, published by the Indian Council for Cultural Relations (ICCR).

Anil Wadhwa was Secretary (East) in the Ministry of External Affairs, and has served as Ambassador to Poland, Oman, Thailand, and Italy. He is a Distinguished Fellow with the New Delhi-based Vivekananda International Foundation. As Secretary (East) in the Ministry of External Affairs of India, he oversaw relations with South-East Asia, the Gulf and West Asia, Pacific and Australasia. He has served as the Indian Ambassador and Permanent Representative to FAO, IFAD, WFP UNESCAP and worked with the Organization for the Prohibition of Chemical Weapons (OPCW) in The Hague heading the Government Relations and Political Affairs and Media and Public Affairs branches. He has led a Confederation of Indian industries task force for writing the Australia Economic Strategy report for the Indian Government released by the Minister of Commerce, Industry & Textiles in November 2020.

Rajiv Bhatia is a Distinguished Fellow at Gateway House since 2016. He served as Ambassador to Myanmar and Mexico and as High Commissioner to Kenya, South Africa, and Lesotho. A former Director-General of the Indian Council of World Affairs (ICWA), he has authored three books – *India in Global Affairs: Perspectives from Sapru House* (KW Publishers, 2015); *India-Myanmar Relations: Changing Contours* (Routledge 2016); and *India-Africa Relations: Changing Horizons* (Routledge 2022).

Dr. Vibha Dhawan is the Director-General of TERI, The Energy and Resources Institute. Dr. Dhawan served as the Vice-Chancellor of TERI School of Advanced Studies from 2005 to 2007. She is a Fellow of the National Academy of Sciences, India. She is a task force member of a number of committees of the Department of Biotechnology (DBT), the Biotechnology Industry Research Assistance Council (BIRAC), the Biotech Consortium India Limited (BCIL), etc. She is currently serving as Adjunct Professor, Consul–General, South Asia Partnership, Michigan State University. She is the winner of several awards, including the Indian Women Achievers Sammaan 2017, Women Leadership Agriculture Award 2016, and the Kamal Kumari National Award for Science and Technology. She has authored six books and over 50 publications.

Pamla Gopaul is Senior Programme Officer, Strategic Initiatives, African Union Development Agency-NEPAD. Gopaul currently serves as a Senior Programme Office for Strategic Initiatives within the Agency and is responsible for the establishment of the Agency's Policy Bridge Tank.

Dr. Nitya Mohan Khemka is Director, Strategic Initiatives at PATH, a global health think-tank focusing on health equity. Nitya is also a visiting Fellow at Judge Business School at the University of Cambridge where she researches topics spanning gender inequality, poverty, and human development, and lectures on sustainable development and gender. A Fellow Commoner for Clare Hall College, Nitya advises the college on its academic programmes and fundraising strategy. She served as co-chair on the health and gender tracks for the T20, the official academic and policy track for the G20 under India's presidency. She serves on the Women's Leadership Board of Harvard's Kennedy School of Government, supporting the Women and Public Policy Program.

Kennedy Mbeva is a Postdoctoral Research Associate in the Global Economic Governance programme. In his role, he is contributing to the Future of Climate Cooperation project, which aims to better understand what institutional changes will be required in order for the international climate change regime, broadly conceived, to meet its objectives.

Dr. Reuben Makomere is a legal adviser at ARIN and a doctoral researcher at the University of Tasmania, Faculty of Law. His current research is focused on governance for addressing ocean acidification through regulation of its response strategies.

Alma Wisskirchen is a political scientist and advisor to the directorate at IDOS, Bonn, Germany.

Acknowledgements

This book is a result of months of experiencing the G20 process first-hand under India's presidency and tracking conferences organised by various think tanks and institutions. The editor of this book is indebted to several diplomats, experts, and institutions for their support, time and guidance. I am grateful to Mr Amitabh Kant, who backed the book by writing an overarching account of India's G20 achievements, based on his keynote remarks at the panel discussion hosted by India Writes Network and Centre for Global India Insights (CGII) in collaboration with the School of International Studies (SIS), JNU.

I am deeply thankful to Mr Harsh Vardhan Shringla, India's Chief Coordinator, G20, and a former foreign secretary, for writing an insightful Foreword to the book that masterfully sums up key facets of India's G20 presidency. His understanding and encouragement kept my spirits high during the editing of this book.

I am deeply grateful to Mr Muktesh Pardeshi, whose organisational skills contributed to the success of India's G20 presidency, for his friendship and unwavering support for this book as well as the special editions of *India and the World*, which formed the basis of this anthology.

I would like to thank all the distinguished contributors/authors who found time to write and update their articles previously published in *India and the World*. This book would not have been possible without them.

Ideas for this book emanated from various conferences and panel discussions we organised on India's G20 presidency in 2023. In this context, I will like to thank institutions who partnered with India Writes Network and CGII in hosting conferences on various aspects of India's G20 presidency. They included SIS, JNU; Vivekananda International Foundation (VIF); Nehru Memorial Museum and Library; Miranda House,

Delhi University and Amity University, Noida. I am thankful to Think20 chair Sujan Chinoy and VIF Director Arvind Gupta, member T20 India, who contributed to our journal as well as this book.

Last but not the least, I am thankful to Pentagon publisher Rajan Arya and his team for steering the publication process.

On a personal note, a special thank you to my wife Shweta and children, Harshvardhan and Poojita, who were weary of my obsession with G20, but were patient and creative with their suggestions that helped improve the look and feel of the book.

Index

Aadhaar, 32, 166

Addis Ababa Financing for Development Declaration, 50, 60

Africa, 31, 40, 75, 78, 81, 88-89, 103, 107-08, 110-13, 119-21, 124, 127-28

African Centre for Disease Control and Prevention, 82

African Continental Free Trade Area (AfCFTA), 89, 111, 117

African Development Bank (AfDB), 82, 123

African Union (AU), 4, 10, 23, 28, 31, 40, 47, 68, 76-78, 81-83, 85, 95-96, 105-06, 109-10, 112, 125

African Union Agenda 2063, 121, 123

African Union Development Agency-New Partnership for Africa's Development (AUDA-NEPAD), 40, 76-77, 123

Agalega, 115

Age of Acceleration, 75

Agenda 2063, 8

Ambassador Jorge Arguello, 92

Amrita Yuva Dharma Dhara (AYUDH), 168

Amritkaal, 42

Andaman & Nicobar Islands, 40

Application Programming Interface (API), 33

Argentina, 37

Artificial Intelligence (AI), 45, 145, 155, 162, 175, 177

Asia, 31, 108

Asia-Africa Conference, 78

Association of Southeast Asian Nations (ASEAN), 10, 37, 107, 127

Atithi Devo Bhava, 185

Atma Nirbhar Bharat, 62

AU's Agenda 2063, 110

Australia, 19, 159

Ayushman Bharat Scheme, 174

Bali, 7, 24, 36, 43, 67, 69, 88, 138

Bandung Declaration, 113

Bangladesh, 39, 102, 107

Banking the Unbankable, 26

Belt and Road Initiative, 113

Beti Bachao, Beti Padhao, 177

Bharat Mandapam, 41

Bharat: Mother of Democracy, 41

Biden, Joe, 110, 145-46

Biofuel Alliance, 15

Boost Institutional Connections, 123

Boston University Development Policy Centre, 154

Brazil, 16, 29-30, 36, 48, 50-52, 94, 136, 156, 179, 181

BRICS, 84, 96, 145, 181-82

Bridging Gender Digital Divide, 64

Brundtland Commission Report, 133

Building a Just World and a Sustainable Planet, 49

C20, 158-61, 168, 170-71

Cambodia, 169

Cameroon, 128

Canada, 159, 180

Capital Adequacy Frameworks (CAFs), 28

CBDR (Common But Differentiated Responsibilities), 33

Central Asia, 90, 127

Chandrayaan-3, 36, 59, 134

China, 12, 16-17, 30, 69, 77, 101, 112-13, 119, 126, 142, 181

China-Africa Cooperation Vision 2035, 113

China-plus-one, 148

Cilliers, Jakkie, 96

Clean Energy, 33

Clean India Mission, 178

Climate Change, 54

Comoros, 25, 40

Compact with Africa (CwA), 77-78, 88

Congo, 111

Connell, Raewyn, 90

Côte d'Ivoire, 87, 121

COVID-19, 3, 11, 14, 16-17, 19, 27, 31, 49, 56, 75, 82, 88-89, 103, 109, 117, 122, 125, 148, 151, 154, 176

COWIN, 27, 32, 176-77

Culture as a Transformative Driver, 194

Cyril Ramaphosa, 88, 96

DAKSHIN (Development and Knowledge Sharing Initiative), 92.106

Data for Society, 162

Debt Resolution, 28

Debt Service Suspension Initiative (DSSI), 7, 89, 121

Delivering Quality Education, 174

Development Working Group (DWG), 15, 76-77, 151

Digital Power, 6

Digital Public Infrastructure (DPI), 26, 45, 68, 115, 128, 155

Direct Benefit Transfer Scheme, 26, 32

Disability, Equity, and Justice, 164

Disaster Risk Reduction, 19, 129

Diversity, Inclusion and Mutual Respect, 166

Domestic Content Requirements (DCRs), 156

e-Arogya Bharti (e-VBAB), 114
ECCE Policy 2013, 173
Education and Digital Transformation, 163
Egypt, 25, 39-40, 102, 121
Empowering Women and Girls, 18
Energy Transitions, 4
e-Sanjeevani, 176-77
Ethiopia, 8, 87, 121
European Union (EU), 86, 112, 119, 128
Event Management Company (EMC), 188
e-Vidya Bharti, 114

Facebook, 17
Financing Sustainable Development, 152
FIPIC (Forum for India-Pacific Islands Cooperation), 107
Food and Agriculture Organization (FAO), 32, 49-50
Forum on China Africa Cooperation (FOCAC), 112
France, 114, 128, 159

G7, 12, 43-46, 67-70, 86, 94, 101, 105, 112, 128-29, 142, 146, 181-82
G20 for All, 38
G77, 85, 113
Gandhinagar, 115
Gaza, 44, 101, 145
GDP (Gross Domestic Product), 101, 109-10, 123-24, 148
Gender Equality, 18, 68, 163
Geographical Indication (GI), 41
Germany, 114, 128, 159
Ghana, 87, 128
Global Biofuel Alliance, 34, 95, 136, 179
Global Digital Public Infrastructure Repository, 155
Global Initiative on Digital Health (GIDH), 176
Global Mobilization to Address Climate Change, 50
Global Security, 118
Global South Centre for Excellence, 106
Global South, 3-4, 8, 11, 13, 17, 21, 23, 27, 29, 40, 43, 47, 51, 76, 78, 84, 86, 94-95, 98-99, 103-08, 110, 126-27, 134, 141, 144, 146-47, 150, 182
Global Sovereign Debt Roundtable, 84
Global Value Chains (GVCs), 139-40
Good Health and Well-Being, 161
Google Pay, 17
Google, 17
Greece, 159
Green Credits Programme, 179
Green Development Pact (GDP), 4, 6, 15-16, 68, 151
Green Finance, 7
Green Skill Development Programme, 179
Gross National Income (GNI), 152
Gujarat, International Kite Festival, 18
Guterres, Antonio, 45, 85, 99, 183

Hamburg Summit, 87
Hangzhou, 77
Har Ghar Jal Initiative, 27
Harvard Business Review, 168
Health and Education, 173

High Level Principles on Lifestyles, 33
Human-centric Globalisation, 102
Hydroxychloroquine, 27

I2U2, 145
Ideas Bank, 34
Independent Expert Group (IEG), 152
India Africa Forum Summit (IAFS), 78
India, 7-8, 10, 12, 17, 19, 23, 28, 30, 33, 37-39, 50, 65, 78, 80, 84, 95, 102-03, 105-08, 113, 115, 119, 127, 134, 136, 148-49, 175-77, 179, 181, 185, 189
India's G20 logo, 37
India-Africa Defence Dialogues (IADD), 115
India-Africa Engagement, 113
India-German Sustainability Development Cooperation, 128
India-Mediterranean-East-Europe-Economic Corridor (IMEC), 44
India-Middle East-European Corridor (IMEEC), 107, 145
Indian Council for Cultural Relations (ICCR), 185-88
Indian Ocean Rim (IOR), 115
Indian Technical and Economic Cooperation Programme (ITEC), 114
India-USA Major Defence Partnership, 145
Indonesia, 30
Indo-Pacific, 44
Institute for Studies in Industrial Development, 154
Intangible Cultural Heritage, 185
Integrated Child Development Services (ICDS), 174
Integrated Holistic Health Working Group (IHH-WG), 161
Integrated Holistic Health, 161
Inter-governmental Panel on Climate Change (IPCC), 118, 133
International Day of Yoga, 54
International Development Association, 153
International Financial Transactions Tax (IFTT), 154
International Labour Organization (ILO), 50
International Monetary Fund (IMF), 8, 13-14, 28, 51, 84, 96, 99, 103
International Solar Alliance (ISA), 33, 134
International Trade Centre (ITC), 140
International Year of Millets, 28, 32
Israel, 159
ISRO, 147
Italy, 43

Jaishankar, Dr. S., 35, 99-100
Jan Bhagidari (People's Participation), 18, 25, 41, 158, 176
Janani Suraksha Yojana (JSY), 174
Japan, 114, 128

Kant, Amitabh, 6, 68, 94, 95
Kashi Culture Pathway, 193
Kenya, 16, 159
Kigali Global Dialogue, 79
Korea, 159

Labour20, 19
Lakshadweep, 40
Laos, 169
Latin America, 31, 90, 103
Least Developed Countries (LDCs), 3, 75, 88, 103, 114
Lending Card, 17
LiFE (Lifestyle For Environment), 33-34, 39, 55, 63, 128, 136-37, 152, 165, 182
Logistics for Trade, 140
Loss and Damage, 46
Lower Mekong River Basin States (LMRBS), 169
Lucknow, 18, 115

Maha Upanishad, 26, 38, 53
Make in India, 148
Malawi, 128
Martin, Paul, 89
Mata Amritanandamayi Devi, 170-71
Mattei Plan for Africa, 45
Mauritius, 25, 39-40, 102, 107, 115
Metaverse, 45
Mexico, 30
Micro, Small and Medium-sized Enterprises (MSMEs), 88, 140
Microsign, 168
Microsoft, 17
Midday Meal Scheme, 173
Middle East, 101, 112
Millet International Initiative for Research and Awareness (MIIRA), 32
Millets and Other Ancient Grains International Research Initiative (MAHARISHI), 28
Ministry of External Affairs (MEA), 128
Model20, 25
Modi, Narendra, Indian Prime Minister, 4, 10, 22, 24-25, 30-31, 33, 35-36, 40-41, 55-56, 58-59, 61, 67-68, 70, 80, 86, 97, 102, 103, 110, 112, 144-47
Morocco, 19, 87
Mozambique, 115
Multilateral Development Banks (MDBs), 68, 97, 126, 152-53, 160
Multi-Year Action Plan on Development, 87
Myanmar, 107

Nagaland, Hornbill Festival, 18
Nari Shakti, 58, 65, 144
National Digital Library, 177
National Early Childhood Care and Education, 173
National Health Mission (NHM), 174
National Rural Landless Employment Guarantee Scheme, 26
Nationally Determined Contributions, 16
Nelson Mandela, 113
Nepal, 107
New Collective Quantified Goal, 7
New Delhi Leader's Declaration, 11, 18, 21, 23, 32, 58-59, 91, 106
New Delhi, 3-4, 10, 31, 34-37, 39-40, 43, 64, 69, 79, 81, 86, 92, 95-96, 105, 145-48, 150, 174
New Development Bank, 126

New India, 24
Nigeria, 25, 39-40, 102
Non-Aligned Movement (NAM), 83, 85, 113
Nour Dados, 90

Oman, 39, 102
One District One Product (ODOP), 41
One Earth, One Family, One Future, 4, 19, 26, 30, 38, 44, 53, 65-66, 70, 79, 80, 103, 129, 133-34, 145, 159, 173, 182, 185
One Future Alliance, 28
One Health, 162, 175
One Sun, One World, One Grid (OSOWOG), 33
Organisation of African Unity (OAU), 110
Organization for Economic Cooperation and Development (OECD), 128, 160
Osaka Summit, 87
Overseas Development Assistance (ODA), 152

Palestine, 51
Palle Srujana, 169
Pan-African E-Network, 114
Partnership for Africa, 45
Paytm, 17
Performing Arts, 189
Peru, 128
Phone Pay, 17
Pine Labs, 17
Planet Earth, 38
Policy Bridge Tank, 123
Portugal, 159
Pradhan Mantri Garib Kalyan Package, 26
Pradhan Mantri Jan Arogya Yojana (PMJAY), 174
Pradhan Mantri Jan Dhan Yojana, 26
Pradhan Mantri Kaushal Vikas Yojana (PMKVY), 173
Production-Linked Incentive (PLI) Scheme, 136, 148
Pro-Planet People (P3), 33

QUAD, 108, 147

Rashtriya Uchchatar Shiksha Abhiyan (RUSA), 173
Reforms and Changes to Policy, 123
Renewable Energy Superpower, 45
Right of Children to Free and Compulsory Education, 173
Rio de Janeiro, 98
River Revival and Water Management, 167
Russia, 9, 12, 69-70, 112, 118-19, 142, 146, 180-81
Russia-Ukraine War, 12
Rwanda, 87

Sabka Saath, Sabka Vikas, Sabka Vishwas, 172
Sall, Macky, 120
Samyukta Arogya, 161
Sarva Shiksha Abhiyan (SSA), 173
Science20, 19
SDG16+ and Enhancing Civic Space, 165
Security, Safety, and Resilience, 162
Self-Help Fund, 129
Self-Reliant India, 62

Semiconductors, The New Oil, 148
Senegal, 87
Seoul Development Consensus for Shared Growth, 87
Seoul Summit, 87
SEWA, 166, 168, 171
Seychelles, 107
Shanghai Cooperation Organisation (SCO), 22
Singapore, 39, 102
Singh, N.K., 14
Small Island Developing States (SIDS), 75, 88
South Africa, 6-8, 25, 29, 36, 40, 82-84, 94, 96, 145, 150, 156
South Asia, 90
South Pacific, 90
Southeast Asia, 90
South-South Agenda, 108
South-South Cooperation, 31, 83
Spain, 39, 102, 159
Sri Lanka, 107
Startup 20 Engagement Group, 20
Sub-Saharan Africa (SSA), 88
Sumangalam, 165
Sustainability and Resilience for Community Engagement and Empowerment (SREE), 170
Sustainable and Resilient Communities, 161
Sustainable Development Goals (SDGs), 4, 6, 9, 13-16, 18, 23, 34, 61, 68, 76, 81, 88, 128, 138, 150-51, 173, 177, 180
Switzerland, 159

Taking G20 to the Last Mile, Leaving None Behind, 36
Tanzania, 115
Tech-equity, 60
Technical and Vocational Education and Training (TVET), 165, 177
Technology for Empowerment, 162
Technology Security and Transparency, 162
Ten-point Action Plan, 63
Thailand, 169
the Caribbean, 127
the Maldives, 107
the Netherlands, 39, 102
Think20, 34, 90, 123
Trade Related Intellectual Property Rights, 155
Trade-Related Investment Measures, 156
Transparency, Trust, and Disinformation, 162
Trilateral Maritime Exercise, 115
Tunisia, 87
Turkey, 19, 119

UAE, 39, 102
Uganda, 113
Ukraine, 9, 44, 47, 51, 69, 101, 112, 118, 146
Ukraine Conflict, 23, 67, 70
UN Framework Convention on Climate Change (UNFCCC), 56
UN's Global Gender Equality Compact, 62
UNESCO World Heritage Sites, 192

UNGA, 32, 51
Unified Payments Interface (UPI), 32, 166
United Kingdom (UK), 114, 119, 128
United Nations (UN), 4, 6, 8, 12, 32, 51, 67, 120, 133, 181, 183
United Nations 2030 Agenda, 138
United Nations Children's Fund (UNICEF), 122
United Nations Conference on Trade and Development (UNCTAD), 99, 118
United Nations Food and Agriculture Organization, 49
United Nations Population Fund, 120
United Nations Security Council (UNSC), 12, 22, 67, 96, 101
Unity of Purpose, 90
Unity of Voice, 90
University Connect programme, 25
UNWOMEN, 61
Upstart, 17
USA, 16, 67, 70, 112, 114, 119, 136, 149, 159, 179

Vaccine Maitri Initiative, 79
Vasudhaiva Kutumbakam, 19, 26, 29-30, 38, 44, 53-57, 66, 79, 103, 109, 129, 133, 145, 159, 171-72, 185
Victory for Global South, 10
Vietnam, 169
Visual Arts, 191
Voice of the Global South Summit (VOGSS), 40, 83, 90, 104-05, 112, 126
Voices of the Global South, 83

WASH, 62
Washington, 145-48
West Asia, 125, 145
West, 9, 43, 95, 146, 181
WhatsApp, 17
Whole-of-country Approach, 37
Why Africa Matters, 111
Women's Empowerment, 163
Women20, 59-60, 63
Woods, Bretton, 126
World Bank, 8, 13, 28, 51, 84, 96, 99, 103
World Economic Forum's Global Risks Report 2023, 18, 95
World Food Programme (WFP), 50
World Health Organisation (WHO), 161, 177
World Meteorological Organization, 95
World Standards Cooperation, 141
World Trade Organisation (WTO), 83, 103, 138-39, 156
World War II, 13, 31

XV BRICS Summit, 9

Youth20, 19
Yuva Samvaad, 25

Zeroda, 17